Churchill Babington

Catalogue of a Selection from Colonel Leake's Greek Coins

Exhibited in the Fitzwilliam Museum

Churchill Babington

Catalogue of a Selection from Colonel Leake's Greek Coins
Exhibited in the Fitzwilliam Museum

ISBN/EAN: 9783742825360

Manufactured in Europe, USA, Canada, Australia, Japa

Cover: Foto ©Thomas Meinert / pixelio.de

Manufactured and distributed by brebook publishing software
(www.brebook.com)

Churchill Babington

Catalogue of a Selection from Colonel Leake's Greek Coins

CATALOGUE

OF A SELECTION FROM

COLONEL LEAKE'S GREEK COINS,

EXHIBITED IN

THE FITZWILLIAM MUSEUM,

BY

CHURCHILL BABINGTON, D.D., F.L.S., &c.

DISNEY PROFESSOR OF ARCHÆOLOGY.

Cambridge:

PRINTED BY C. J. CLAY, M.A. AT THE UNIVERSITY PRESS.

1867

INDEX.

				PAGE
Division I.	Coins of Kings and Dynasts			6
„ II.	„	Asiatic Greece		16
„ III.	„	Continental Europe (excluding Italy)		26
„ IV.	„	Europe continued; Italy and Sicily		34
„ V.	„	Islands of the Roman, &c. African Greeks		44
Note on the weights of Greek Coins				49

CATALOGUE

OF A SELECTION FROM

COLONEL LEAKE'S GREEK COINS,

EXHIBITED IN

THE FITZWILLIAM MUSEUM.

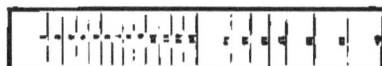

Size of the Coins.   *Scale of Mionnet.*

N. B. The tickets in the glass-case, nearly the whole of which are written by Col. Leake, are placed above the coins to which they refer; and the following Catalogue is designed as much as possible to afford information in addition to what they supply. Consequently the types and legends are not ordinarily described at length. The denominations of value, as stater, tetradrachm, &c. are usually added for the gold and silver coins; but the values of the copper coins are for the most part unknown. These last indeed, to speak generally, appear to be rather tokens than coins proper, and so not to be adjusted with accuracy to any scale; the coinages of Italy, Sicily, and Egypt offer some exceptions to this remark. The whole question, however, of denominations and scales is at present in a perplexed and uncertain state. The brown tickets indicate that the coins below them are electrotypes, being impressions in most cases of very rare or finely preserved originals. The abbreviations AV, EL, AR, ÆK, which occur on the tickets stand for aurum, electrum, argentum, and æs, indicating the metal of which the coin is made, whether gold, electrum, silver, or copper. The figures on the tickets refer to the sizes of the coins, and are taken from the scale of Mionnet which is given above. The weight of the gold and silver coins is also added in grains Troy; the weight of the copper (or brass) coins being in general not given, because coins in this metal (which varies somewhat in coins of different places) have usually lost more in weight than those in other metals. The abbreviation ℞ on the tickets is used for the *reverse* or back view of the coin; R or L often stand for

"to the right" or "to the left," i.e. to the right or left of the spectator. Thus on ticket n. 2 "Horseman R" means that the horseman is moving toward the spectator's right hand: on ticket n. 23, "Head Perseus L" signifies that the head is facing towards the left hand of the spectator. *Ex.* is an abbreviation for *exergue*, or the lower part of the reverse, which is divided from the rest by a straight line, or otherwise. See no. 60, &c. The open space of a coin is called its field, designated ƒ on the tickets, see no. 13, &c.; upon it are often found adjuncts i.e. secondary types, or monograms, the meaning of both which can only in comparatively few cases be discovered. When Col. Leake's ticket reads "another similar," it indicates that his cabinet contains another specimen of the same coin; in such cases a fuller description is added in this Catalogue. In printing the Greek legends no attempt has been made to imitate the ancient forms of the letters.

Col. Leake's divisions of coins into classes is here followed, though it would have been much better if he had simply followed Eckhel, who arranges the coins of Kings, not apart by themselves, but in connection with the regions over which they reigned. Thus the coins of Macedonia in genere, and the coins of the various cities of Macedonia, are in Eckhel's system, now almost universally adopted, viewed in juxtaposition with those of the Kings of Macedonia. In Col. Leake's *Numismata Hellenica*, which is the printed Catalogue of his collection, will sometimes be found information, which is not contained either on the tickets or in this Catalogue. To this, a copy of which is kept in the Library, the reader is referred.

1

FIRST DIVISION.

Coins of Kings and Dynasts.

A. Europe.

1. *Kings of Macedonia.*

1 **Alexander I.** (Reigned about B.C. 500—454). *Obverse.* Male figure, wearing the Macedonian hat (causia) and light cloak (chlamys), bearing two spears, walking behind a bridled horse. *Reverse.* Sunk square, usually called 'quadrate incuse,' including another square of four divisions, around which is the legend ΑΛΕΞΑΝΔΡΟ.

R. M., on Leake's ticket, indicates that the original of this very rare piece is in the British Museum. If the Alexander of this coin is Alexander I. of Macedon, as is generally assumed, it is the earliest regal coin known to us having a legend. Some of the Darics (see n. 84 in this selection) may perhaps be as old, but they bear no inscriptions. With the types and weight of this coin compare one of the Orrescii in Thrace (n. 90 of European Greece). It is difficult to speak with certainty about the scale of the old Macedonian coinage before Alexander the Great; many, as L. Müller, consider it to be Eginetan, and call n. 10 a didrachm or two-drachm piece of that scale. Col. Leake however seems to have reason to doubt the correctness of this view, and rather inclines to suspect it to be of the Euboic standard, whose unit (or dram) appears to have been from 53 to 57 grains Troy. (The Eginetan drachm, as determined from coins of Ægina, is about 93 grains troy.) In this view n. 10 is a tetradrachm (four-dram piece) and the present coin an octodrachm. The octodrachm or eight-dram piece is of very rare occurrence, and surpassed in weight only by certain pieces of Athens (*Europ. Greece,* n. 24) and Sicily (n. 73, 128—132 in this selection). In Queipo's view it is a hexadrachm of a system which he calls Olympic; he recognises also another system, which he calls Bosporic, in the Macedonian money before Alexander, whose drachms weigh about 73, and 57 grains Troy, respectively. (*Essai sur les systèmes métriques et monétaires,* Vol. I. p. 144. Paris, 1859.) His Olympic may perhaps be considered as reduced Eginetan, and his Bosporic as Euboic weight.

It will be observed that the reverse presents a transition from the rough incuse of the earliest coins (see n. 84 below, and nos. 70, 71, 80, 81 in Asiatic Greece in this selection) to the later coins in which the reverse has a fully developed type of its own. The termination of the genitive, O and not OY, seems to be universal before the age of Philip II., in whose reign the other form first appeared, as it seems, and became speedily almost universal, though lingering traces of the older form are found as late as Lysimachus.

2 **Archelaus** (B.C. 413—800). Perhaps a light tetradrachm; see previous remarks.

This coin has no legend, but a similar one in the British Museum reads ΑΡΧΕΛΛΟ. The goat, which gave the name to the Macedonian capital *Ægæ,* previously called Edessa, refers to the legend of Caranus (see Leake *Num. Hell. Kings,* p. 1), and was the symbol of the Macedonian empire (Dan. viii. 5). The advance in art on this coin as compared with the last deserves notice, the types of the obverse being nearly similar.

3 **Do.**, the coin reading ΑΡΧΕΛΛΟ. Denomination doubtful: possibly a tridrachm, more probably a very heavy didrachm.

The youthful head, having the diadem, is considered by some to be young Hercules, by others to be Apollo. It is not a portrait of Archelaus, for no regal portraits appear on coins before the age of the successors of Alexander.

4 **Amyntas II.** (B.C. 303—369). Same denomination. The original is in the British Museum.

5 **Do.** Same denomination, but lighter. *Obr.* Head of Hercules in lion's scalp to right. *Rev.* ΑΜΥΝΤΑ. Horse to right.

6 **Do.** This is among the earliest Greek copper coins.

7 **Philip II.** (B.C. 359—336). Gold didrachm, or stater. (Attic scale).

8 **Do. Do.**

These beautiful gold coins of Philip, which had a wide circulation down to Roman times, are peculiarly interesting as being the prototype of the early British gold coinage. (See British and English coins in this selection, n. 1,

&c.) They were worth 20 Attic silver drachms, i.e. about 20 francs.

Scarcely any European gold is earlier than Philip II. The head of the obverse is most probably Apollo; the biga, or two-horse chariot of the reverse, commemorates Philip's Olympian victories. See *Num. Hell.* (Kings), p. 3. The adjuncts (the thunderbolt on n. 7 and the trident on n. 8) indicate the places of mintage on the coins of Philip and succeeding kings: the thunderbolt is probably for Pella, and the trident for Amphipolis. See L. Müller's *Monnaies de Philippe II.* nos. 1 and 59.

9　Do. Half-quarter stater. The cantharus is more especially the cup of Bacchus, and is often seen in his hand. See a vase in case III. In this Museum.

10 and 11　Do. Tetradrachm and didrachm (Euboic scale?). Both struck at Pella.

12　Do. Copper coin. *Obv.* Head of Apollo (or young Hercules) to right. *Rev.* Horseman, below a monogram. Place of mintage uncertain.

13　Alexander III. (B.C. 336—323). Gold tetradrachm or double stater, with the thunderbolt for Pella. (Müller, n. 4).

14　Do. Stater. The gold stater or didrachm of Alexander the Great had an immense circulation, and was struck in a great many cities both of Europe and Asia, and the same may be said of his silver tetradrachms (nos. 16, 17).

In Müller in his *Numismatique d'Alexandre Le Grand* (Copenhagen, 1855) enumerates between 1700 and 1800 varieties of the coins of Alexander, the greater part of which are gold staters, and silver tetradrachms, and drachms; differing from each other only in the adjuncts; from which the place of mintage can sometimes be determined. The present coin is n. 633 of Müller, and is considered to belong to Northern Greece, the precise place being uncertain.

15　Do. Quarter stater. The bow and club relate to Hercules.

16　Do. Silver tetradrachm. *Obv.* Head of Hercules in lion's scalp to right. *Rev.* ΑΛΕΞΑΝΔΡΟΥ ΒΑΣΙΛΕΩΣ, Jupiter sitting on a throne.

Below throne ΚΑ; in the field a monogram. Struck according to Müller (n. 717) in Northern Greece.

The silver as well as the gold money of Alexander the Great is adjusted to the Attic scale; the gold money only of Philip being so adjusted. The Attic drachma properly weighs about 67 grains Troy; but the tetradrachms of Alexander vary in weight considerably, being sometimes heavier, more usually lighter than this standard. In the following pages, by tetradrachm, drachma, stater, &c., the Attic tetradrachm, &c. is intended, the contrary not appearing.

17　Do. Do., reading ΑΛΕΞΑΝΔΡΟΥ only,

The arms of the throne of the reverse of this rare variety terminate in winged Victories, which on some other coins, has no back but more usually a back with plain arms. The figure in the field is believed by L. Müller to represent a dancing Apollo holding the sacred fillet in both hands, being probably a copy of a statue of an Apollo in some temple at Sicyon, where this coin is considered to have been struck. (Müller, n. 860, p. 219.)

18　Philip III. (Aridæus) (B.C. 323—316). Gold stater, types those of Alexander (n. 14). The ΛΥ in the field of the reverse indicates, in L. Müller's opinion, that the coin was struck in Lycia. (*Monnaies de Philippe III.* n. 96.)

19　Demetrius Poliorcetes (B.C. 294—287). Tetradrachm, on the obverse of which is his portrait. The Neptune, holding an acrostolium, of the reverse, alludes to the naval victory gained by his father Antigonus and himself over Ptolemy Soter in Cyprus, B.C. 306. Very fine work.

20　Lysimachus (B.C. 288—280). Gold stater. *Obv.* Portrait of Alexander the Great, as the young

Ammon, with the ram's horn. *Rev.*
ΒΑΣΙΛΕΩΣ ΛΤΣΙΜΑΧΟΤ. Pallas
holding a victory, seated, her shield
behind. In the field, torch and
monogram.

Struck at Chrysoris (*i. e.* Stratonicea) in
Caria, according to Müller, *Münzen des Lysimachus*, p. 82 (Copenhagen, 1858); who refers
to this identical coin of Leake.

21 Do. Tetradrachm, same types,
but a different monogram. Müller,
n. 401, who thinks it was struck
at Sigeum. Fine work.

22 Do. Drachma or dram. Types of
the silver coins of Alexander the
Great; the throne of Jupiter has
no back.

The lion and crescent in the field perhaps
indicate that this coin was struck at Cardia in
Thrace, over which country Lysimachus had
previously reigned soon after Alexander's death;
similar adjuncts occur on a coin of Alexander.
(Müller, *Alex.* n. 358, *Lysim.* n. 19.)

23 Antigonus Gonatas (B.C. 283—239).
Tetradrachm.

The head of Pan, in the centre of the Macedonian shield of the obverse, alludes to the
defeat of the Gauls at Delphi by Antigonus
(B.C. 279); that God having been supposed to
have struck them with a panic. The Pallas of
the reverse is probably a copy of the archaic
statue in the temple of Pallas Itonia between
Larissa and Pherae, for the forked drapery, &c.
is foreign to the age of Antigonus, and (except
in cases of affected archaism) peculiar to the
early period of Hellenic art.

24 Philip V, (B.C. 220—178). Didrachm; the original is in the
British Museum, as is indicated
by the B.M. of the ticket.

25 Do. Tetradrachm. The head of
the hero Perseus in the centre of
the Macedonian shield on the
obverse (who has the *harpe* or
hook behind his neck), alludes to
Philip's assumed descent from
Perseus; after whom he named
his son and successor.

Leake thinks that we have here the portrait of Philip V. as Perseus; but this seems
doubtful, if we compare this coin with his un-
doubted portrait on n. 24.

26 Perseus (B.C. 178—167). Tetradrachm. *Obv.* His portrait (of
beautiful work) to right; below in
small letters ΖΩΙΛ[ΟΤ], standing,
as is thought, for Zoïlus, the artist
who cut the die. *Rev.* ΒΑΣΙΛΕΩΣ
ΠΕΡΣΕΩΣ. An eagle standing on
a thunderbolt, enclosed in wreath
of oak; in the field a monogram.

It is not certain that Zoïlus was the artist;
he may have been a magistrate. At the same
time the names of magistrates usually occur
on the reverses of coins, though there are certain exceptions to this remark, *e. g.* coins of
Apollonia in Illyricum have the names of magistrates on both sides. See remarks on n. 15
of Asiatic Greek coins in this selection.

2. *Kings of Epirus.*

27 Alexander I, son of Neoptolemus
(B.C. 342—325). Gold stater of
very fine work, thought to have
been struck at Tarentum, in Italy,
which was succoured by Alexander against the Lucanians and
Bruttii, about 335 B.C. The oak
wreath on the head of Jove shows
that he is the Jove of Dodona.
The thunderbolt of the reverse
may be compared with the coins
of Agathocles. See Div. IV. n. 137.
The original is in the Hunterian
Museum at Glasgow.

28 Pyrrhus (B.C. 312—272). Gold
drachma.

This beautiful coin is presumed to have
been struck at Syracuse about 278 B.C., when
Pyrrhus was fighting with the Carthaginians
in Sicily. The type of the obverse resembles
a coin of Syracuse. See Div. IV, n. 111.

29 Do. Didrachm.

The type of the reverse resembles the gold
coins of the Bruttii, see Div. IV, n. 1; and this
coin is conjectured to have been struck in their

territory, perhaps at Consentia, when Pyrrhus visited Italy (280—274 B.C.) to aid the Italian Greeks of Tarentum and other cities against Rome. Fine work.

30 Do. Tetradrachm, of very beautiful work, thought to have been struck at Syracuse.

A clever forgery of this magnificent coin has been executed by Becker.

31 Do. Drachma, also thought to be of Syracusan work. Compare the coins of Syracuse. Div. IV. n. 136, 138. Probably of the Æginetan scale, but light; (Persian, according to Queipo.)

32 Alexander II. of Epirus, according to Leake. (Began to reign B.C. 272.) Tetradrachm, Ptolemaic scale.

The attribution of these beautiful coins is uncertain. Leake's arguments in favor of Alexander II. of Epirus may be seen at great length in *Num. Hell.* (Kings), p. 18. Against them is the well ascertained fact that they are principally found in Egypt; and other able numismatists, as Cousinéry, Pinder, and L. Müller, think that they were struck in Egypt in honour of the deified Alexander the Great by Ptolemy Soter. The ram's horn on smaller coins of this type (see n. 33) greatly confirms the view that we have on the obverse the head of Alexander the Great as the young Ammon bound with the diadem (see n. 20), clothed also with the elephant's scalp, as the conqueror of India. The Reverse, reading ΑΛΕΞΑΝΔΡΟΥ, has Pallas Itonia apparently (compare n. 28), which it is difficult to connect with Ptolemy or Alexander the Great, though easy, as Leake shews, to explain in reference to Alexander II. of Epirus, whose father Pyrrhus dedicated the shields of the Gauls in the temple of Pallas Itonia. Notwithstanding upon the whole Müller's opinion seems most probable; and it may be added that Pallas Itonia occurs on Bactrian regal coins. (See n. 89.) Müller calls her simply Athene Promachus.

33 Do. Drachma. Types nearly as before, but the *corn* Ammonis appears on the head of Alexander. Scale as before.

3. *Dynasts of Paeonia.*

34 Patraus. (Contemporary with Philip II. or nearly so.) Perhaps a tetradrachm of the Greco-Asiatic scale. See nos. 1 and 2.

The Macedonian shield in the hand of the fallen foe, shews that Patraus is earlier than Alexander, who reduced Paeonia to submission B.C. 335. He seems to be unknown to literary history; Leake thinks he is "contemporary with or earlier than Philip II."

He cannot be much if at all earlier, as the genitive of his name ends in OT on his coins. See remark at the end of n. 1.

35 Audoleon. (Began to reign probably about B.C. 350, was certainly reigning B.C. 310.) Same denomination.

The monogram of the reverse, AT, may be for the commencement of his name.

B. KINGS OF ASIA.

1. *King of Asia.*

30 Antigonus (B.C. 311—301). Tetradrachm; fine work.

The type of Neptune on the obverse and of the galley on the reverse seem to allude to his victory over Ptolemy Soter in 306. See n. 19.

2. *Seleucidae, or Kings of Syria.*

On the obverse of this beautiful series of regal coins we very generally have portraits of the reigning sovereign. The reverses relate principally to the worship of Jupiter and Apollo, sometimes also to Pallas, the Dioscuri &c. From the reign of Antiochus III. downwards the larger silver coins are usually dated; the era being that of the Seleucidae, which commenced in the autumn of 312 B.C. when Seleucus and Ptolemy Soter defeated Demetrius Poliorcetes at Gaza.

37 Seleucus I. (Nicator) (B.C. 312—280). Gold stater. The original, formerly in the Duke of Devonshire's collection, is now in the British Museum.

All the gold coins of the Seleucidae are excessively rare; strangely contrasting in that respect with the plentiful gold coinage of Philip and Alexander. The genuineness of all the gold octodrachms (see n. 40) in this series has been doubted, but without sufficient reason.

38 Do. Tetradrachm of the same type as Alexander's, on both sides. (See n. 16.)

Lysimachus also, in his earlier coinage, copied the types of Alexander: see n. 22.

39 Do. Tetradrachm, but of different types.

The anchor in the field of the reverse was the signet of Seleucus I. and occurs frequently on coins of the Seleucidæ, from whence it passed over to the coins of the Jews under the Maccabees. He adopted it in consequence of a vision in which his mother appeared to him (Appian. *Syr.* 56).

40 Do. Copper coin. *Obv.* Head of Pallas. *Rev.* ΒΑΣΙΛΕΩΣ ΣΕΛΕΥ-ΚΟΥ. Victory crowning the name of Seleucus; before her an anchor.

41 Antiochus I. (Soter) (B.C. 280—261). Tetradrachm.

On some few coins with this type and portrait Antiochus is styled *Soter*. The *cortina* (curtain) drawn over Apollo's tripod is seen also on many other coins of this series.

42 Antiochus II. (Theos.) (B.C. 261—246). Tetradrachm.

There is great difficulty in assigning many coins which only read ΒΑΣΙΛΕΩΣ ΑΝΤΙΟΧΟΥ or ΒΑΣΙΛΕΩΣ ΣΕΛΕΥΚΟΥ to their proper owners; the portraits being the principal guides, and uncertain ones withal. This coin, remarkable for its winged diadem, which is attributed by Leake to Antiochus II., is by other numismatists considered to belong to Antiochus Hierax, his younger son.

43 Seleucus II. (Callinicus) (B.C. 246—226). Gold stater.

44 Do. Tetradrachm.

45 Seleucus III. (Ceraunus) (B.C. 226—223). Tetradrachm.

46 Antiochus III. (Magnus) (B.C. 223—187). Gold octodrachm.

The original of this almost unique coin was in the Pembroke collection, and it was considered to be genuine by Mr. Burgon. It

fetched however, together with a tetradrachm of the same king, only £7. 12s. See *Pembroke Catalogue,* p. 241.

47 Do. Gold stater.

Mr. M. Borrell has noted respecting this specimen, " Poor, but appears genuine." See remarks on n. 37.

48 Do. Tetradrachm.

The monogram in the field which reads into T. T. P. shews that this coin, like many others of the Seleucidæ, was struck at Tyre. The date ΔΡ *i. e.* 104 of the Seleucidæ = 208 B.C. when this coin was struck.

49 Seleucus IV. (Philopator) (B.C. 187—175). Tetradrachm.

50 Antiochus IV. (Epiphanes) (B.C. 175—164). Tetradrachm of rare type (having the head of Jove) and beautiful work.

Antiochus Epiphanes is the first of the Seleucidæ, who styles himself *God* upon his coins; none succeeding monarchs as Demetrius II., Cleopatra (mother of Antiochus VIII.), Demetrius III. and Tigranes followed his example. This act in itself would make him appear peculiarly odious to the Jews, of whom he was the relentless persecutor.

51 Do. Tetradrachm of the ordinary types bearing his portrait, and a representation of the Jove of Olympia by Phidias on the reverse.

Antiochus IV. caused a copy of the Olympian Jove to be executed of the colossal size of the original, and to be placed at Daphne.

52 Do. Copper coin, of unusually large size.

The types, style, and size of this piece are similar to many copper coins of the Ptolemies. There can be no doubt that Antiochus struck it in Egypt in one or other of his four campaigns in that country (171—168 B.C.).

53 Antiochus V. (Eupator) (B.C. 164—162). Tetradrachm, (Attic, but light).

This king was only nine years old at his accession, and was murdered by Demetrius two years afterwards; the artist who engraved this rare coin has made him appear like a grown man.

54 Demetrius I. (Soter) (B.C. 162—150). Tetradrachm. *Obv.* Portrait of the king wearing his diadem, within a wreath. *Rev.* Seated female to left holding in her right hand a wand, a horn of plenty in her right ; on both sides of her in three lines ΒΑΣΙΛΕΩΣ ΔΗΜΙΙΤΡΙΟΤ ΣΩΤΗΡΟΣ (King Demetrius the Saviour); in exergue ΑΞΡ (Year 161 Sel. *i.e.* 151 B.C.).

This fine coin is from the Thomas collection.

55 Do. Copper coin (with animal types).

These serrated coins appear to be of copper only, and are tolerably frequent in the series of the Seleucidæ, but scarcely, it is believed, occur in any other. The Romans however had serrated denarii, which, as Tacitus informs us, were known to the Germans and used by them. The attribution of the copper coins of the Seleucidæ to their true owners is peculiarly uncertain, unless they are accompanied by portraits; three kings bearing the name of Demetrius reigned at no long intervals from each other.

56 Alexander I. (Bala) (B.C. 150—146). Fine tetradrachm.

57 Antiochus VI. (Dionysus) (B.C. 146—137). Tetradrachm.

The TPT. in the field stands for Tryphon, who was chief minister of his father Alexander Bala, and brought the son forward as a claimant of the crown against Demetrius Nicator. The OP is 170 Sel. *i.e.* 142 B.C.

58 *Do. Drachm. *Obv.* Head of Antiochus VI. radiated (in the character of Apollo) to *r.* *Rev.* Apollo seated on his *cortina* to *r*, holding bow and arrow. Same legend, with a monogram : in exergue ΟΞ. ΣΤΑ.

59 Tryphon. (B.C. 142—139). Tetradrachm. *Obv.* King's portrait to *r.* *Rev.* Macedonian helmet, an ibex horn projecting in front ;

on the body of the helmet are ornamentations (eagle and winged lion apparently, in circular compartments); the cheek-piece has a thunderbolt for ornament, in the field a monogram. Electrotype from the original in the Hunterian Museum at Glasgow.

The silver tetradrachms of Tryphon, the minister and murderer of Antiochus VI. are among the rarest in this series, only about four or five being known. The Pembroke specimen, now in General Fox's cabinet, fetched £130.

60 Demetrius II. (Nicator) (B.C. 146—125, with interruptions). Tetradrachm, dated ΙΞΡ, 167 Sel. *i.e.* 145 B.C.

61 Antiochus VII. (Euergetes, or Sidetes) (B.C. 137—128). Tetradrachm.

62 Do. Tetradrachm, with type of Tyre on reverse. (See Div. II. n. 109. Tyre). Date ΖΟΡ, year 177 Sel. *i.e.* 135 B.C. Scale Ptolemaic.

Not only is the eagle &c. the same as on the Tyrian tetradrachms, but a monogram ending in the club of Hercules reads Τ. Τ. Ρ. and another monogram reads Α Σ Τ. for *douleu the inviolable*. P.E.A. in two lines is for *iepâ the sacred*. Coins of the Seleucidæ struck at Tyre and Sidon are mostly of the Ptolemaic scale; nearly all the rest are Attic, but often light.

63 Demetrius II. Returned from captivity B.C. 120. Tetradrachm. Date 194 Sel. *i.e.* 128 B.C.

The head of the obverse, called on the ticket Jupiter, though with a mark of doubt, is more usually considered to be the portrait of Demetrius himself, after his return from captivity, and Col. Leake himself in the *Num. Hell* (Kings), p. 32, adopts this view.

64 Alexander II. (Zebina) (B.C. 128—122). Tetradrachm.

65 Do. Serrated copper coin.

The attribution must be regarded as uncertain (see remarks on n. 55). The copper coins ascribed to Alexander Bala have the same legend, and on one of them is a head of Bacchus, as here. See *Num. Hell* p. 28.

66 Cleopatra, mother of Antiochus VIII. (Reigned alone, B.C. 125). Tetradrachm, dated ZHP. 187 Sel. i.e. 125 B.C.

The ΘΕΑΣ ΕΤΕΠΙΡΙΑΣ of the reverse taken in connection with the veil of the portrait shews that Cleopatra is represented in the character of Ceres, as goddess of Abundance. The type of the reverse is Egyptian (see nos. 99, 100), as is not unnatural, Cleopatra being daughter of Ptolemy VI. (Philometor). The original of this most rare coin, now in the British Museum, fetched at Lord Northwick's sale £240.

67 Cleopatra and Antiochus VIII. (Grypus) (B.C. 124 — 121). Date 180 Sel. i.e. 123 B.C.

From the Pembroke collection, where it fetched £13.

68 Antiochus VIII. (Reigned alone, B.C. 121 — 96). Tetradrachm of very fine work, and in perfect preservation.

The first letter of the date is "off the coin" in the exergue of the reverse, in consequence of the flan of the coin not having been sufficiently spread out to contain it; ϙΡ (190) being the only letters whose tips are visible; consequently the coin, though lying between 122 and 112 B.C., cannot be dated more precisely.

69 Do. Tetradrachm, struck at Tarsus, bearing on the reverse the representation, as is generally supposed, of the tomb of Sardanapalus, who was buried there.

This type occurs on the coins of Tarsus (see Div. II. nos. 98—100), but its meaning is uncertain. It seems to be a sepulchral monument, but Lenke tries to shew, *Num. Hell.* (Asia), p. 128, that it is probably not the tomb of Sardanapalus.

70 Antiochus IX. (Philopator or Cyzicenus) (B.C. 125—95). Tetradrachm with bearded portrait.

71 Antiochus X. (Eusebes). (B.C. 95—83, or thereabouts). Tetradrachm of rather rough work, as those of the Seleucidæ now most usually are, as well as of light (Attic) weight.

72 Antiochus XI. (Philadelphus) (B.C. 95). Tetradrachm of rough work.

73 Philip (Reigned about B.C. 94—84). Tetradrachm.

The execution of this coin, though rather coarse, is much better than Philip's usual coinage, which is often quite barbarous.

74 Tigranes (B.C. 83 — 69). Tetradrachm, struck at Antioch in Syria.

The king's portrait on the obverse has the tiara of Armenia, of which country he was also king. The figure of the reverse represents the Fortune or City of Antioch, as a woman setting her foot on the river Orontes (personated by a boy swimming). For further remarks see the coins of Antioch (Div. II. nos. 5 and 6).

3. *Princes of Judæa.*

75 Alexander Jannæus (B.C. 105—78). *Obv.* "Jonathan the High Priest and the Confederation of the Jews" in Samaritan character within a wreath. *Rev.* Two horns of plenty and a poppy-head.

The coins previously given to Jonathan Maccabæus are now generally assigned to Alexander Jannæus (Madden's *Jewish Coinage*, p. 84).

76 Herod the Tetrarch (Antipas) (B.C. 4—A.D. 39). Date ΛΖ 37. The date is probably his regnal year, and is the same as that of the Christian era, which begins four years too late.

This coin, like most or all of the other coins of Herod Antipas, was struck at Tiberias, a city founded by him near the lake of Gennesareth, in honour of Tiberius (Madden's *Jewish Coinage*, p. 98).

77 Herod Agrippa I. (A.D. 37 — 44). *Obv.* BACIΛΕΩC [ΑΓΡΙΠΑ] around an umbrella, a symbol of regal dignity. *Rev.* Three wheat-ears springing from one base; in field, the date ϛ, or year 6, i.e. 41 A.D. (Madden's *Jewish Coinage*, pp. 104—106).

This coin, formerly given to Agrippa II, is now assigned to Agrippa I. ('Herod the King,' Acts xii.).

4. *Kings of Bithynia.*

78 Nicomedes II., son of Prusias II. (B.C. 149—91). *Obv.* His portrait (with diadem) to right. *Rev.* ΒΑΣΙΛΕΩΣ ΕΠΙΦΑΝΟΥΣ ΝΙΚΟΜΗ-ΔΟΥ. Jupiter crowning the name of Nicomedes; in his left hand a sceptre, with eagle before him: near his feet a monogram, and the date ΚΣ, 205. Remarkably fine; formerly in the Devonshire cabinet.

The era on the coins of the Kings of Bithynia is the same as that of the Kings of Pontus, and commenced 297 B.C. The present coin was consequently struck 92 B.C.

5. *Kings of Pergamus.*

79 Uncertain king. Tetradrachm. *Obv.* Head of Philetærus. *Rev.* ΦΙΛΕΤΑΙΡΟΥ. Pallas seated, with spear, shield, and bow.

The kingdom of Pergamus was founded by Philetærus, keeper of the treasures of Lysimachus, in 280 B.C., who held it till 263 B.C.; it lasted till 133 B.C., when Attalus III. left it to the Romans by will. The legend of the kings of Pergamus is always ΦΙΛΕΤΑΙΡΟΥ, and the portrait is nearly always the same; so that the coins have never been assigned satisfactorily to any of the kings; though some of them have the monogram of Eumenes, of whom there are two.

80 Uncertain king. Do. The same types and legend, but the portrait differs.

This is presumed by Leake to be the portrait of Attalus II., the legend notwithstanding. *Num. Hell.* (Suppl.) p. 7.

6. *Kings of Galatia.*

81 Amyntas (contemporary of Cicero). Tetradrachm. *Obv.* Head of Pallas to right. *Rev.* ΒΑΣΙΛΕΩΣ ΑΜΥΝΤΟΥ. Victory moving to left, holding sceptre with ribbons.

Compare the coin of Sida. Div. II. n. 84.

7. *Kings of Pontus and Bosporus.*

82 Mithradates the Great (Eupator) (B.C. 120—63). Tetradrachm of the finest work. *Obv.* Head of Mithradates VI. to right, the diadem visible above. *Rev.* ΒΑΣΙΛΕΩΣ ΜΙΘΡΑΔΑΤΟΥ ΕΥΠΑΤΟΡΟΣ. Stag feeding; star and crescent before it. In field two monograms and date ΔΚΣ, 222 – 75 B.C. The whole enclosed in a wreath of ivy leaves and berries.

83 Rhoscuporis III. (contemporary of Caracalla). Stater of Electrum or pale gold, dated ΑΙΦ, year 511 = 214 A.D.

The kings of the Bosporus and their dates are known to us in great measure from their coins. Some are as late as the fourth century. "La taille de ces monnaies est fort remarquable, puisqu'elle n'appartient à aucun des systèmes connus." Queipo table XLI, who further remarks on their affinity with the Cyzicene staters, which seem to have been the gold currency of the Bosporus. This coin weighs nearly half a Cyzicene stater. See Div. II. n. 21.

8. *Kings of Persia.*

84 Uncertain king. *Obv.* King as archer, to right. *Rev.* Oblong punch-mark, with shapeless impression.—The Daric.

The Daric is commonly said to be so called after Darius son of Hystaspes (B.C. 521—485), though it may be derived with at least equal probability from a Persian word, signifying king. It seems to have been coined by the Persian monarchs for circulation over their own dominions and over Greece proper, while the empire lasted. The heads differ somewhat on different specimens, and some ingenious rather than successful attempts have lately been made in France to recognise in them portraits of the different Persian kings.

This coin is usually thought to be intended by 'dram' in the books of Ezra and Nehemiah; if so, it is the only coined money named in the Old Testament, the shekels, &c. being only weights. For the scale see note at the end, § 4.

2

85 Same types in silver.—The Aryandic, or unit of the Persian scale.

Arryandes, the Persian governor of Egypt, is said to have imitated the gold Daric of Darius, son of Hystaspes, in silver; a piece of presumption, which cost him his life, according to Herodotus. It was notwithstanding adopted, and like the Daric had a very wide circulation; being still commonly met with in Asia Minor.

86 Uncertain king, probably Artaxerxes II. (Mnemon)(B.C. 405—359). *Obv.* Portrait of the king, in a cap with flaps. *Rev.* ΒΑΣΙΑ. and Lyre.

This is considered by Col. Leake (*Num. Hell. Kings,* p. 53) to offer a portrait of Artaxerxes I. (Longimanus) (B.C. 465—425); but Mr Newton prefers to regard it as a portrait of the second king of that name. In either case, it is the earliest portrait which occurs on a coin. It is far from certain however that it is a portrait at all; coins of Lampsacus have a very similar head. See Div. II. p. 51, 52. (The latter is doubtless Bacchus.)

9. *Kings of Bactriana.*

This kingdom was made independent of the kings of Syria about 255 B.C. by Diodotus, governor of Bactra (Balkh). We have in the series of Bactrian coins a number of kings (Greek, Indo-Scythic, &c.) down to Mahommedan times, some of which are only known to us by their coins. Their chronology is to some extent conjectural only. Wilson's views in his *Ariana Antiqua* are here mostly followed. See also *Numism. Chron.* for 1857. Vol. XIX. p. 13.

87 Euthydemus. (Began to reign about 220 B.C.). Tetradrachm.

He may be considered the founder of the greatness of the Bactrian kingdom. His son Demetrius married a daughter of Antiochus the Great.

88 Eucratides (B.C. 180—150, more or less). Tetradrachm.

A Macedonian helmet, similar in form to the one here worn by Eucratides, was found a few years ago in the bed of the river Zab.

89 Menander. Reigned about 125 B.C. Tetrobol, apparently; (hemidrachm, according to Wilson).

The Arianian legend of the reverse is, *Maharajasa Tadarasa Minandasa.*

90 Do. Square copper coin, having the same Greek and the same Arianian legend as the preceding.

The square coins, both in silver and copper, are almost peculiar to the Bactrian series.

91 Azes. (Reigned probably about 60 B.C.) Tetrobol, apparently.

The Arianian legend of the reverse is, *Maharajasa Mahatasa Ayasa.* The coins of this king are extremely numerous both in silver and copper.

92 Kadphises. (Reigned probably about 90 A.D.) Double stater or gold tetradrachm.

The figure alongside the Indian bull on the reverse is Siva. The king's dress, as seen on this and the following coin, shews that he is of Tartar or Scythian race, who notwithstanding encouraged the native religion of India.

93 Do. Copper coin.

This coin is curiously re-struck (*recusus*). The Greek legend of the obverse (around Kadphises, standing) ought to be ΒΑCΙΛΕΤC ΒΑCΙΛΕΩΝ (CΩΤΗΡ ΜΕΓΑC ΟΟΗ) ΜΟ ΚΑΔΦΙCΗC, but the letters between brackets are obliterated by nine Arianian letters, belonging to the reverse of a similar coin. Similarly on the reverse the Greek letters ΛΕΤC ΒΑCΙΛΕΩ appear among the Arianian letters.

94 Kanerkes (Reigned probably in the second or third century A.D.) Copper coin.

The name and figure of the Sun on the reverse, and the fire-altar on the obverse of this and the preceding coin shew that these Indo-Scythian kings had adopted the Persian fire-worship, as well as the Indian superstitions.

. C. AFRICA.

Kings of Egypt. (*Lagidæ.*)

95 Ptolemy I. (Soter) (B.C. 323—285). Gold pentedrachm, (five-drachm piece.)

The serpents, by which his ægis (or decorated cloak) is confined round the neck are, seen before and behind. The scale of the coins of the Ptolemies is termed Lagid by Queipo, but it scarcely differs from the early Macedonian money adjusted to a scale, which he calls Bosporic, and which Leake suspects to be Euboic. See n. 1. Queipo makes the Lagid drachma 3.54 grammes (= 54.6 grains Troy); and the Bosporic drachma 3.71 grammes (= 57.2 grains Troy).

96 Do. Gold hemidrachm.

97 Do. Silver tetradrachm with the title of Soter, and various letters in the field.

This coin being undoubtedly of the first Ptolemy helps to fix the attribution of other coins, which read only ΠΤΟΛΕΜΑΙΟΥ ΒΑΣΙΛΕΩΣ, having a similar portrait.

98 Ptolemy II. (Philadelphus) (B.C. 285—247.) Gold octodrachm.

This remarkable coin gives on the obverse the portraits of Ptolemy Philadelphus and his wife Arsinoë, with the legend ΑΔΕΛΦΩΝ, *brother and sister*, Arsinoë being also his sister: the reverse gives portraits of their deceased parents, Ptolemy Soter and Berenice, who are styled *gods* (ΘΕΩΝ). The portrait of Ptolemy Soter on this coin may be compared with nos. 95 and 97. The original of this electrotype is in the British Museum. (Col. Leake has accidentally written the description on an uncoloured ticket.) Some consider this coin to have been struck by Ptolemy III. in honour of his predecessors; but it seems more likely to have been executed by order of Ptolemy II.

99 Arsinoë, sister and wife of the preceding. Silver decadrachm or ten-dram piece.

The flower at the top of her head is probably the lotus. The reverse gives the double horn of plenty, or *διδύμος*, a vessel invented in her honour as goddess of plenty twice-told. (Athenæus p 497). As respects the legend, ΦΙΛΑΔΕΛΦΟΥ is an adjective agreeing with ΑΡΣΙΝΟΗΣ, not a substantive depending upon it.

100 Do. Gold octodrachm. Same types.

101 Ptolemy III. (Euergetes.) (B.C. 247—221.) Gold octodrachm.

The obverse appears to indicate that Ptolemy Euergetes assumed the attributes of three divinities, as he wears the ægis of Pallas, (whence issues a serpent,) holds the trident of Poseidon, (the central prong of which is ornamented with the lotus,) and in fine wears on his head the radiated crown of Apollo or the Sun.

102 Berenice II., wife of Ptolemy III. according to Leake. Gold hemidrachm, Attic scale.

It is not certain to what Berenice this rare little coin should be assigned. Col. Leake purchased it at the sale of the Pembroke collection for the somewhat small sum of £5. 2s. 6d. Mr Burgon (*Pemb. Cat.* p. 273) thinks that the coin was struck in Syria "in consequence of the weight being adjusted to the Attic and not the Ptolemaic talent." The coin now weighs nearly 33 grains, and is therefore half the Attic drachma, whose full weight is computed by Col. Leake to be 67.5; whereas the Ptolemaic drachma must have weighed about 54 or 55 grains. Well preserved tetradrachms of Ptolemy Soter weigh about 220 grains (see n. 97, and compare the weights of the gold octodrachms which sometimes reach about 429 grains.) "The stars would point to Tripolis as the place of mintage, where the Dioscuri were prominently the tutelary divinities." (Burgon.) See Div. II. n. 105 (Tripolis). On some of the gold octodrachms of Arsinoë, which are certainly not adapted to the Attic talent, we have the club and monogram of Tyre.

103 Ptolemy V. (Epiphanes) (B.C. 205 —181.) Gold octodrachm.

For the two stars, see remarks on the preceding coin.

104 Ptolemy XII. (Dionysus) (B.C. 51 —47). Silver didrachm.

From the Pembroke collection, where it fetched £8. 12s. 6d.

105 Cleopatra, sister of Ptolemy XII. (B.C. 51—30). Tetradrachm of base silver, adjusted to the Attic

2—2

talent, as debased in Roman times.

The place of mintage of this curious piece is unknown; but it was most likely not in Egypt; more probably in Asia. Cleopatra appeared in public, as Plutarch tells us, in the character of the New Isis; which explains the legend of the obverse, ΘΕΑ ΝΕΩΤΕΡΑ. The legend of the reverse, ΑΝΤΩΝΙΟC ΑΥΤΟ-ΚΡΑΤΩΡ ΤΡΙΤΟΝ ΤΡΙΩΝ ΑΝΔΡΩΝ, is the Greek rendering of Antonius Imperator III. Triumvir. Thus, as Col. Leake observes, this coin was struck B.C. 35, when Cleopatra was in her 34th year, and Mark Antony about 53 years of age. Perhaps this coin gives as faithful a portrait of Cleopatra as is known, but she has been unfortunate in her artists. The lunar epsilon and sigma are early examples of their kind.

106 Do. A denarius, and properly belonging to the Roman series of coins.

Portraits of Cleopatra and Mark Antony as before, and of better execution, but that of Cleopatra is on a very small scale. The legends, as Leake remarks, prove that the coin was struck after Antony's return from Armenia, B.C. 34, when he and Cleopatra publicly invested one of their sons with the attributes of King of Armenia and Media, and the other with those of King of Phoenicia, Syria, and Cilicia. On the legend of the obverse, Filiorum Regum must be taken in apposition with the preceding Regum, so that Cleopatra styles herself Queen of kings, who are sons of kings (i. e. of herself and Antony). For the Armenian tiara behind the head of Antony, compare n. 74 (Tigranes).

107 Do. Copper coin of herself only.

This coin is evidently by its fabric one of the Egyptian series. With the three portraits of Cleopatra here given may be compared Div. II. n. 108 (Tripolis), on the obverse of which, as many think, Antony and Cleopatra are represented in the characters of the Dioscuri: it has unfortunately suffered a good deal by circulation.

DIVISION II.
ASIATIC GREECE.

1 Abydos? Hecta or sixth part of the Cyzicene stater, generally supposed to be struck at Abydus. Obv. Head with curved horn. Rev. Eagle. No legend.

This coin, as well as No. 4 and Nos. 72—76 in this division, and n. 41 in Div. III. were found in a supplemental cabinet of Col. Leake, which contained various other coins of doubtful attribution, or in an unsatisfactory state of preservation. They are not described in the Numismata Hellenica, and the tickets accompanying those which are here exhibited are written by the author of this catalogue.

2 Aradus in Phoenicia, (Arvad of the Old Testament, now Ruad). Tetradrachm.

The ΓΚΡ of the reverse is the date, 123. The era of Aradus commenced B.C. 259, when its independence was probably guaranteed by a treaty between the kings of Syria and Egypt. Consequently the present coin was struck B.C. 136. Below the date is a Phoenician letter, and below that two Greek letters whose meaning seems to be unknown. The turreted and veiled head of the obverse is probably a personification of the city (compare the coin of Antioch, n. 5, Seleucia, n. 81, Sidon, n. 86, and Tripolis, n. 105).

3 Do. Drachm. Obv. Bee, and two monograms. Rev. ΑΡΑΔΙΩΝ. Stag and palm-tree.

The types on both sides are the same as those of Ephesus (see n. 25); and the coin was most probably struck there indicating an alliance between Aradus and Ephesus.

4 Do? Octodrachm. Obv. King in chariot of oriental style; his charioteer in front, an attendant behind on foot. Rev. Galley and Phoenician letter.

These fine coins are thought by some to be struck at Aradus, and during the time of Persian supremacy over Phoenicia; or between the age of Darius son of Hystaspes and that of Alexander the Great (B.C. 521—336). The galley and Phœnician letter appear to indicate a coast-town of Phœnicia. The scale is Phœnician, or Bosporic (i.e. Euboic); see below Div. v. no. 69.

5 Antioch of Syria, of Augustus. Tetradrachm of reduced Attic scale, apparently. (Bosporic, according to Queipo.

The obverse gives a good portrait of Augustus, and the reverse is the fortune or city of Antioch personified (a woman sitting her foot on the neck of a swimming boy, who symbolises the river Orontes. Comp. Div. i. o. 74). This was the composition of Eutychides of Sicyon, and the statue was contained in a temple (τυχείον) which is seen in n. 6. The same composition, a little varied, is repeated on the reverses of imperial coins of other cities of Asia, e g. Samosata and Tarsus. See K. O. Müller, *Ancient Art and its Remains*, § 15n. The legend of the reverse, ΕΤΟΥΣ ΙΙΚ ΝΙΚΙΗΣ, "the 28th year of the victory," refers to the battle of Actium, the Actian era commencing B.C. 31. The present coin was therefore struck B.C. 3 (or, as Leake says, B.C. 4). The ΤΙΙΑ IB refers to the 12th consulship of Augustus; and the ATT. to the autonomy of Antioch, ΤΙΙΑ. ATT. being expressed in monograms. Queipo thinks that no coins of Antioch are adjusted to the Attic scale; an improbable hypothesis, seeing that the kings of Syria struck nearly all their money thereby.

6 Do. of Trebonianus Gallus and Volusian (A. D. 251—254). See preceding remarks.

S. C. in the exergue is for Senatus Consulto; the legends of the coins of Antioch being often partly in Latin, partly in Greek; as well as in Greek only or in Latin only. The meaning of ΔΕ "cannot be readily explained." (Leake).

7 Alexandria in the Troad. Tetradrachm.

The ΑΠΟΛΛΩΝΟΣ ΖΜΙΘΕΩΣ of the reverse indicates the statue to be that of Apollo Smintheus (for the orthography see Leake, *Num. Hell.*) who destroyed the rats with his arrows. ΑΛΕΞΑΝ. of the exergue is for ΑΛΕΞΑΝΔΡΕΩΝ, which occurs at length on other coins of this city, and PMA in the field is the date 141. Leake thinks that the era dates from the fall of Antigonus, B.C.

300, and that the date of this fine and rare coin is consequently B.C. 159.

8 Antioch of Caria, of Gallienus (A. D. 253—268). *Obv.* AT. K. ΙΙΟ. ΓΑΛΛΙΗΝΟC. Bust of the Emperor Gallienus to l. *Rev.* ΕΠ. ΑΡΧ. ΑΦ. ΑΝΤΙΟΧΕΩΝ. i.e. when Aphrodisius was archon. (See *Num. Hell.*) The river Mæander personified as a recumbent figure on a bridge; behind him is a man walking; to the left are arches with a square superstructure (possibly of an aqueduct); below the arches of the bridge the river flows rapidly; fishes are seen below.—Large brass.

The bridge of the Mæander at Antioch of Caria, mentioned by Strabo, was on the great eastern road from Ephesus. See Leake for details.

9 Aspendus in Pamphylia. *Obv.* Two wrestlers opposed. *Rev.* ΕΣΤFΕΔΙΙΤΥΣ being the Pamphylian form of the name Aspendus. Slinger discharging his sling. In the field a triscelium; below φ, and a wild goat, as countermark below. Persian didrachm.

For the language of the legend, see Leake. The triscelium (or three-leg-piece) occurring also on the coins of Sicily, and in modern times on those of the Isle of Man, may probably be a religious symbol; it does not seem to have been explained. The countermark is the stamp of some other state to make the coin pass current there; Leake observes that it resembles the Cretan wild goat.

10 Bithynian Confederation in the reign of Hadrian (A.D. 117—138). *Obv.* Portrait and titles of the Emperor Hadrian. *Rev.* Temple of eight Corinthian columns, with ΚΟΙΝΟΝ across the field, in exergue ΒΕΙΘΥΝΙΑC.

Confederations for religious and political purposes, perhaps based on earlier ones, existed in many parts of Asia in imperial times. With these various officers were connected;

r. g. the Κοινὸν Ἀσίας, or Commune Asiæ (i. e. Proconsular Asia) had its Asiarchs and its High-Priests of Asia; and similarly the Commune Bithyniæ had its Bithynarchs. The temple may be supposed to represent (conventionally, probably) the sacred building employed by the Confederation. The metal of this coin is yellow brass, which is by no means usual.

11 Byblus in Phœnicia, of Macrinus (A.D. 217, 218). *Obv.* Portrait and titles of the Emperor Macrinus. *Rev.* ΙΕΡΑC ΒΥΒΛΟΥ. Temple of eight columns, surmounted by a tall pyramid; behind it a square enclosure or portico; (the temple of Venus and burial-place of Adonis); on the left is a temple (of Isis) of two columns, at the entrance an altar.

See Leake, *Num. Hell.*, and Donaldson's *Archit. Numism.* p. 105, n. 30.

12 Cibyra in Phrygia, of Macrinus. Medallion of unusually large size.

The era of Cibyra commenced A.D. 24, the year after an earthquake. The date 193 thus corresponds to 217 A.D. The sacred casket (κίστη) on the head of the priestess is said to be connected with the name of the city.

13 Cæsarea of Cappadocia (prius Mazaca), of Trajan. (A.D. 98—117.) Double denarius. *Obv.* ΑΥΤ. ΚΑΙ. ΝΕΡΟΤΑC ΤΡΑΙΑΝΟC CΕΒΑC. ΓΕΡΜ. Head of Trajan to right. *Rev.* ΥΠΑΤ. ΔΕΥΤ. (i. e. Cos. II.) Statue of Apollo on the summit of Mount Argæus.

Trajan's second consulate was A.D. 98, when this coin was struck. Mount Argæus, at the base of which the city lay, was regarded, according to Maximus Tyrius, as a deity. The name of the city is omitted on many (not all) of its coins, but the type removes all doubt as to the attribution.

14 Clazomenæ of Ionia. Gold coin of very fine work.

This coin seems to be the third part of the stater of Phocæa, which weighs about 254 grains.

15 Do. Tetradrachm of very fine work, with the same types of Apollo and the Swan; but with ΘΕΟΔΟΤΟΣ ΕΠΟΕΙ ("Theodotus made it") on obverse.

The number of coins which have a legend, distinctly stating who engraved the coin, is very small indeed. Another example is a coin of Cydonia in Crete, ΝΕΥΑΝΤΟΣ ΕΠΟΕΙ. But there is a larger number which have proper names in small letters, which are usually thought to be the names of the artists. See Div. i. n. 26, &c. The reverse of this coin doubtless had ΚΛΑΖΟ, but it is "off the coin," the metal not being sufficiently beaten out.

16 Do. Very early coin.

The weight of this coin is singular, and it may possibly be a very light didrachm of the Euboïc scale. Mr Burgon remarks that its weight is half the gold stater of the same place, which differs from the Cyzicene. (Thomas Catalogue, p. 290.) Early Asiatic gold and silver coins rarely, it is believed, belong to the same scale.

17 Do. Hemidrachm, (Attic scale); types in 14 and 15.

18 Cnidus of Caria. Drachma. *Obv.* Head of Venus to right, hair in a knot behind: behind the neck a monogram. *Rev.* ΚΝΙ. ΤΕΛΕΑΣ. (magistrate's name.) Head and foreleg of lion.

Venus, who was especially worshipped at Cnidus, is commonly placed on its coins.

19 Cyme of Æolis. Tetradrachm of fine work.

The adjunct, a vase of peculiar form, on the reverse occurs frequently either as a primary or secondary type of coins of Cyme, but hardly anywhere else.

20 Do. of Tranquillina, wife of Gordian III. (She was reigning A.D. 241.) *Obv.* ΦΩΤΡΙΑ ΤΡΑΝΚΤΑ-

ΑΕΙΝΑ ΣΕΒ. **Her portrait.** *Rev.* E. ΑΤΡΙ. ΑΣΚΛΗΠΙΑΔΟΥ ΓΡ. (γραμματέως) ΚΤΜΑΙΩΝ (the last four letters in the field.) The Ephesian Diana, half-stags at her feet. See n. 30, &c.

This coin well illustrates Acts xix. 27. "The great goddess Diana...whom all Asia and the world worshippeth." Her image also occurs on coins of Acraeus in Lydia, of Ancyra in Phrygia, &c. The town-clerk is a functionary mentioned on various other coins of Asia, e.g. Ephesus. See Acts xix. 35.

21 Cyzicus of Mysia. Stater of electrum or pale gold, the alloy of silver being about one fourth.

The Cyzicene staters are mentioned by Demosthenes and others, and were reckoned equal to 28 Attic silver drachmæ; their normal weight being about 218 grains. Their types are various, but the tunny fish is generally present, as here: they are almost always without legends.

22 Do., according to Leake. The third part of the Cyzicene stater.

Countermarks occur on the face and edge of this coin, which however seems not to have been struck at Cyzicus; the quadrate incuse of the reverse is very different, and resembles that of Sardes, n. 80, 81, which has moreover in part the same type. It is impossible to speak with certainty of the place of mintage of many of these early uninscribed gold and electrum coins.

23 Do. Hecta, or sixth part of the Cyzicene stater.

The attribution of this coin to Cyzicus may be considered certain, as the tunny fish occurs upon it.

24 Ephesus of Ionia. Very early silver coin, drachma (Greco-Asiatic scale).

The Muses in the guise of bees led a colony from Athens to Ephesus, according to Philostratus and Himerius.

25 Do. Attic Drachma. *Obv.* Bee between ΕΦ. *Rev.* ΝΙΚΟΛΟΧΟΣ

(magistrate's name): stag and palm-tree.

The stag was sacred to the Ephesian Diana, and sometimes is represented at her feet both on coins of Ephesus and elsewhere. See n. 20.

26 Do. Didrachm (Greco-Asiatic) of beautiful work. *Obv.* Head of Diana (quiver behind). *Rev.* ΕΦ. ΠΥΘΑΓΟΡΑΣ (magistrate's name), bee, and half-stag.

The Diana of the obverse is the true Artemis, who was strangely identified both by Greeks and Romans with the many-breasted Asiatic deity of fecundity, who was worshipped at Ephesus especially and also very widely throughout Asia. See n. 20.

27 Ephesus of Ionia. Cistophorus.

The Cistophorus is mentioned by Cicero and other ancient writers. It is a tetradrachm of the "Greco-Asiatic" (Queipo) (or "Rhodian" Pinder) scale, whose unit or dram is three fourths of the Attic scale, so that the Cistophorus would pass for an Attic tridrachm in countries where that scale prevailed. It is a coin peculiar to the kingdom of Pergamus, or (as it afterwards became) the Roman Proconsular Asia; the era of which began B.C. 133, when Attalus III. bequeathed his kingdom to Rome. The present coin being dated 53 was consequently struck B.C. 80. The types of the Cistophorus refer to the mystical worship of Bacchus; the obverse has the mystic chest, from which a serpent emerges; the reverse has two serpents with an object between them which on the best executed specimens is seen to be a bow-case; but it is usually only very partially represented. This is also an attribute of Bacchus. In later times the Romans modified the type (n. 28), or retained the denomination and abolished the type. This very interesting class of coins has been made the subject of an ample monograph by M. Pinder (*Ueber die Cistophoren und über die Kaiserlichen Silber medaillons der Romischen Provinz Asia*. Berlin, 1856, from which some of these remarks were derived. See Nos. 28, 30, 31, 51, 68, 104 in this Division. Whether the Greco-Asiatic scale be identical with what was anciently termed the Rhodian, or (as Queipo thinks) its half only, seems uncertain.

28 Do. Cistophorus. *Obv.* **M. ANTO-
NIVS IMP. COS. DESIG. ITER. ET. TERT.**
Head of Mark Antony within an
ivy-wreath. *Rev.* **III VIR R. P. C.**
(*i. e.* Triumvir Reipublicæ consti-
tuendæ). Mystic cista between
serpents; above it the head of
Octavia. Struck before B.C. 34.
(Eckhel vI. 65, Pind. t. 2. f. 1.)

For other portraits of Antony, see Div. I.
Nos. 105 and 106.

29 Do., according to Leake, Didrachm, or double denarius of Nero
(A.D. 54—68) of base silver. *Obv.*
**NEPΩNOC KAICAPOC ΓEPMANI-
KOΣ.** Young bust of Nero to
right. *Rev.* **ΔIΔPAXMON** Simpu-
lum and lituus. (Augur's sacri-
ficial vessel and staff.)

The place of mintage, though not named,
is probably Ephesus. (See Finder, p. 577.) This
is one of the very few coins on which the denomination is inscribed. In imperial times the
drachma was debased to the level of the denarius, so that this is in fact a double denarius.

30 Do. of **Claudius** (A.D. 41—54).
Cistophorus medallion.

31 Do. of Hadrian (A.D. 117—138).

32 Do. of Septimus Severus (A.D.
193—211). Large brass.

With the Ephesian Diana, as seen on these
three coins, compare that seen on n. 20.

33 Do. of Trajanus Decius (A.D. 249
—251). Small brass.

The reverse has the river-god, Cayster, re-
cumbent, and bearing his name. River-gods
are commonly represented as holding a reed
in one hand, and having by their side an urn
from which water flows.

34 Do. of Gallienus (A.D. 253—208).
Middle brass.

The legend of the reverse **EΦECIΩN Δ.
NEΩKOPΩN** implies that Ephesus was ap-

pointed temple-warden (νεωκόρος) of the empe-
rors for the fourth time, an honour conferred on
Ephesus only, whence the legend on a coin of
Elagabalus, **EΦECIΩN MONΩN AΠACΩN
TETPAKIC NEΩKOPΩN.** Ephesus is called
in Acts xix. 35, worshipper (temple-warden) of
Diana, which is illustrated by an Ephesian coin
of Caracalla and Geta reading **EΦECIΩN
TPIC NEOKOPΩN (sic) KAI THC APTE-
MIΔOC.** The type of the reverse, which
Leake scarcely understood, is Fortune holding
the Ephesian Diana, in allusion to the pro-
sperity of the city as depending on her goddess.

35 Do. of Do. Small brass.

The Diana of the reverse is not the Ephesian Diana, though the two were identified.
See n. 26. Greek imperial coins (*i. e.* which
have an emperor's head on one side, and which
are in fact the Greek coinage of the empire)
terminate with the reign of Gallienus, to speak
generally. (The *Nummi Alexandrini* are a
notable exception to this remark.)

36 Erythræ of Ionia. Olympic drachma. *Obv.* Male figure holding horse.
Rev. Full-blown flower in quadrate incuse, in the angles EPTH.

The weights of the coins of Erythræ of
about this size vary very considerably. See
the following coin, and Leake's *N. Hell.*

37 Do. Bosporic drachma, apparently.

The principal types on both sides (head
in lion's scalp, and club and bow-case) refer to
Hercules; the owl on the reverse to Minerva,
his patron-goddess. Their temples at Erythræ
are mentioned by Pausanias. See Leake, *N. H.*

38 Do. Copper coin, with the same
principal types.

39 Do. Copper coin.

The **EPTΘPAI** of obv. indicates that the
turreted bust is meant for the city personified.
The 'bosom-fire,' as Leake calls it, of the reverse is curious.

40 Eucarpeia of Phrygia, of Septimus Severus (A.D. 193—211).
Large brass.

The usual representation of Health, feeding
a serpent from a saucer (φιάλη).

41 Mausolus, satrap of Halicarnassus (B.C. 377—353).

42 Hidrieus, satrap (B.C. 351—844).

43 Pixodarus (B.C. 341—335).

The types of these coins of these satraps or tyrants of Halicarnassus are the same. *Obv.* Head of Apollo or the Sun seen in front. *Rev.* Jove holding sceptre and double axe (λάβρυς). About their denominations it is less easy to speak ; the weights seem to agree best with what Queipo calls the Eruporic scale. Brandis however calls their scale Rhodian ; Queipo regards it as "attique, quoique affaibli en général."

44 Heliopolis of Cœle-Syria, of Septimius Severus (A.D. 193—211). Middle brass.

The reverse shews the great temple of Jupiter at Baalbec seen in perspective. Like the other beautiful buildings still standing there it seems to be of the second century after Christ. On the upper part of the coin are to be seen traces of I. O. M. H. (which Leake has omitted) i.e. Jovis Optimi Maximi Heliopolitani. These letters, according to Sestini, occur frequently on the coins of the city from Sept. Severus onwards.

45 Timotheus and Dionysius, tyrants of Heraclea in Bithynia, in the time of Alexander the Great. Olympic didrachm. (Weight omitted by Leake. Lord Northwick's specimen, which fetched £16, weighed 146 grains.)

The head of the obverse with a thyrsus behind is probably of a Bacchante, (not of Bacchus, as Leake says).

46 Shekel of Simon Maccabeus struck at Jerusalem (B.C. 144—135). *Obv. Shekel Israel* (in Samaritan characters), i.e. The shekel of Israel. A cup: above it two letters for *Shenath Shethaim*, i.e. year 2. *Rev. Jerushalaim ha-kedoshah,* i.e. Jerusalem the Holy. A triple lily.

About B.C. 139 Antiochus VII. granted to Simon liberty to coin money with his own stamp (1 Macc. xv. 2—9). These shekels are now almost universally considered to belong to Simon, and the numerals to refer to the years of his coinage. The type of the obverse has been very frequently taken for the pot of manna, and that of the reverse for Aaron's rod that budded ; but against this view see Madden's *Jewish Coinage*, pp. 48, 49. More probably both types are simply a cup and a lily, and express the prosperity of Judæa ; compare the expression of O. T. " my cup shall be full ;" " Israel shall blossom like a lily " (Hos. xiv. 5). The coin is in fact a tetradrachm of the Ptolemaic (" Lagid," Queipo) scale ; Josephus, by a slight inaccuracy, identifies the shekel with the Attic tetradrachm. De Sauley, *Num. Jud.* p. 25.

47 Ilium in the Troad. Tetradrachm.

The reverse gives a representation of Minerva Ilias, whose temple was at New Ilium. The threads hanging down from her distaff may be noted. Formerly in the Pembroke collection, now in that of Gen. Fox.

48 Jewish copper coin of Augustus. Quadrans or farthing (St Mark xii. 42).

The date L AΘ, year 39, is probably the year of Augustus, which began, according to Censorinus, Jan. 1, 727 (B.C. 27) ; in which case this coin was struck A.D. 12, when M. Ambivius was procurator. This and the two following coins are of the class which are supposed to be struck by the procurators. See Madden's *Jewish Coinage*, pp. 134—138, 301.

49 Similar coin of Tiberius. Farthing.

The date of the coin 17, is A.D. 30, which was therefore struck when Pontius Pilate was procurator or governor, who held office A.D. 25—35.

50 Similar coin of Nero. Farthing.

The year 5 of Nero, or A.D. 58, when this coin was struck, is the last year but two of the procuratorship of Claudius Felix.

51 Lampsacus in Mysia. Gold didrachm.

The head may possibly be that of Artaxerxes Mnemon. See Div. I. n. 86.

52 Do. Tetradrachm.

3

The type of the reverse is Apollo Musageles, i.e. *Conductor of the Muses*, in a long robe, holding the lyre and plectrum. He was so represented at Actium in his temple, and Eckhel thinks that this coin was struck in reference to the victory of Augustus over Mark Antony at Actium, B.C. 31. The date of the coin can hardly be very much earlier, as appears by the lunar sigma and epsilon. Compare a coin of M. Antony and Cleopatra, Div. I. n. 105.

53 Laodicea in Syria. Tetradrachm of Bosporic scale, according to Queipo.

Jupiter holding a Victory occurs on the reverse of coins of the Seleucidæ. See Div. I. n. 50, 56, &c. It is sometimes difficult to distinguish the Bosporic and the reduced Attic scales. See n. 82, and remarks on coins of the Seleucidæ, Div. I. p. 9.

54 Laodicea in Phrygia. Cistophorus. (See n. 27.)

55 Do. Cistophorus medallion of Hadrian. *Obv.* HADRIANVS AVGVSTVS P. P. His head to right. *Rev.* cos III. Jupiter of Laodicea holding eagle and sceptre, as on coins of Laodicea in Phrygia. (Figured in Pinder's *Cistoph.* t. VIII. f. 1, whence the defects in Leake's description are supplied.) Hadrian was consul for the third time A.D. 119, and so remained ever afterwards.

56 Lebedus in Ionia. Tetradrachm, of fine work.

57 Magnesia in Ionia. Tetradrachm.

58 Do. Do., same types, but with a different magistrate's name.

The beauty of the draped bust of Diana on the obverse and of the figure of Apollo on the reverse of these coins can hardly be exaggerated. The original of n. 57 was in Lord Northwick's collection, at whose sale it realised the extraordinary sum of £263. No. 58 is in the British Museum.

The symbol of the Mæander, near whose banks this Magnesia was built, is also used for other rivers, and occurs frequently as an orna-

ment of Greek vases, as may be seen by the collection in this Museum; in modern art it is sometimes called the key-ornament.

59 Mallus in Cilicia. Double Aryandic, or didrachm of Persian scale.

Evidently struck under Persian influence; see Div. I. nos. 84, 85. "These coins of Mallus are strong indications that it was the principal sea-port of the Persian government in Cilicia, prior to the time of Alexander." (Leake.)

60 Miletus in Ionia. Didrachm, of Greco-Asiatic scale. *Obv.* Laureated head of Apollo to left. *Rev.* Lion looking back at a star, MI in monogram (Miletus); in exergue ΕΡΓΙΝΟΣ.

The temple of Apollo at Branchidæ near Miletus explains the type of the obverse. The lion and star refer to the sign of the Zodiac; similarly a ram looks back at a star on coins of Antioch in Syria.

61 Mopsuestia in Cilicia, of Valerian (A.D. 253—260). First brass. *Obv.* ΑΤΤ. Κ. ΟΤΑΛΛΕΡΙΑΝΟC CЄΒ. Head of the Emperor Valerian to left. *Rev.* Five-arched bridge over the Pyramus; under each arch a letter of the word ΔΩΡΕΑ; on the bridge a river-god reclining, a gate at each end. ΑΔΡ. ΜΟΨΕΑΤΩΝ ΓΚΤ (323 of the Pompeian era = A.D. 256); in exergue ΠΤΡΑΜΟC.

(Legends taken from Leake, *N. H. Suppl.* p. 69; but the date seems to be ΚΤ, i.e. 320 = A.D. 253.)

The word δωρεά seems to indicate that Valerian built this bridge over the Pyramus; in the following century Constantius built another.

62 Myrhina in Æolis. Tetradrachm. *Obv.* Head of Apollo to right. *Rev.* ΜΤΡΙΝΑΙΩΝ. The Grynean Apollo sacrificing; in his right hand, saucer (phiale); in his left, branch with pendent fillets; in the field a cantharus and the cortina, and a monogram; all within wreath.

Apollo's temple at Grynium was about six miles from Myrina.

63 Nacrasa in Lydia. Small brass coin. *Obv.* ΘΕΟΝ CΥΝΚΛΗΤΟΝ (*sc.* ἡ πόλις τιμᾷ). Head of the Roman Senate personified, to right. *Rev.* ΝΑΚΡΑCΙΤΩΝ. The Ephesian Diana and Stags.

See remarks on n. 20 and nos. 30—32.

64 Nagidus in Cilicia. Didrachm (Persian scale).

65 Do. Do., fine work.

Eckhel thinks the type of the reverse is Jupiter rather than Bacchus; if so, one may suspect the reverse to be intended for Juno. Leake calls it " Venus crowned, like Juno."

66 Neapolis in Samaria (now Nablous), of Macrinus (A.D. 217, 218). *Obv.* [ATT. K. M.] ΟΠ. CE (Opelius Severus) ΜΑΚΡΙΝΟC CEΒ. Head of the Emperor Macrinus to right. *Rev.* ΦΛ. (Flaviæ) ΝΕΑC. ΠΟΛΚΟC CΤ[ΡΙΑC]. Mount Gerizim; upon it a temple of Jove of four columns; at the foot of the mountain a portico, from whose centre steps rise to the summit; on a peak of the mountain a smaller temple.

The Samaritan temple, built about 334 B.C. in honour of Jehovah, on Mount Gerizim, was in the time of Antiochus Epiphanes consecrated to Jupiter, lest the Samaritans should suffer persecution like the Jews. It was destroyed by Hyrcanus; but Damascius speaks of a temple of Jupiter there at a later period. It was probably built not very long after the destruction of Jerusalem, as it is represented on coins of Hadrian and later emperors. The city called itself Flavia in honour of Titus and Domitian.

67 Perga in Pamphylia. Tetradrachm.

The goddess on both sides of this coin is the Artemis of the Greeks, whom they identified with the Diana of Perga; she is represented however on other coins of Perga as a veiled statue with a modius on the head. The same identification was adopted as regards the Ephesian deity. See nos. 26, 30—32, and remarks.

68 Pergamum, or Pergamus, in Mysia. Cistophorus.

One of the monograms reads ΠΕΡ. for Pergamus; the other is for ΠΡΥΤ. (Prytanis), followed by ΒΑ. (the first letters of his name). The cistophori of Pergamum are much more common than those of any other city, and somewhat more numerous.

69 Do. Small copper coin.

The Pergamus of the obverse must be a magistrate, whose name coincided with that of the city; which was said to have a hero Pergamus (Πέργαμος κτίστης on coins) for its founder.

70 Phocæa. Stater of electrum, or pale gold.

The Phocæan staters are mentioned by Thucydides and Demosthenes, but they are now among the rarest of Greek coins; they are of purer gold and about six grains heavier than the Cyzicene staters (see n. 21). Staters of Phocæa and their Hectæ (sixth parts) are also named in an inscription of the British Museum. The Phoca or seal occurs as the type of the stater, and the secondary type of its hecta (no. 71).

71 Do. Hecta of the stater, adjunct a seal.

72 Do. Uncertain hecta, probably of Phocæa, as there seems to be a trace of a seal to the left of the bearded head.

73—78 Uncertain hectæ of Asiatic cities, some of very beautiful work; all uninscribed.

The accompanying tickets are by the compiler of this catalogue; the coins were not included by Leake in his *Numismata Hellenica* in consequence of their uncertain attribution. A great number of them are figured as *aurei incerti* by Sestini in his *Descriz. degli Stateri antichi.* (Fir. 1817.) They appear to be of the fourth and fifth centuries B.C. (those

3—2

with the quadrate incuse on the reverse being the oldest), and to belong to cities on or near the west coast of Asia Minor. They are all about size 2 (or rather less), and weigh about 40 grains.

79 Sardis in Lydia, according to Leake. Hecta of the stater.

Omphale, daughter of Jardanos, king of Lydia, wore the club and lion's skin of Hercules, while he under the influence of Love handled the distaff. Omphale so attired occurs on one inscribed coin of Sardis; hence the attribution of the present coin.

80 Sardis. Gold coin probably adjusted to the Babylonian talent, but equivalent to the Attic didrachm.

This coin appears to be the original shekel of Phœnicia, thence derived to Lydia. The heads of the lion and bull facing bespeak an oriental origin.

81 Do. Silver coin of the same types, but of a lower weight. Siclos of Xenophon.

This is the drachma or unit of the Persian silver scale of Queipo, and like the Aryandic (Div. 1 n. 85) weighs about 86 Troy grains. Though called *siglos* (i.e. shekel) by the Greeks, the original Phœnician or Babylonian shekel, the named of Egypt, was equivalent to the Attic didrachm. See Leake's note (in *Num. Hell.*) on the *Weights of Greek coins*. Both this and the preceding are among the earliest coins known, and may probably be of the time of Crœsus (b.c. 560—546), or thereabouts. Those in silver are tolerably common; the gold pieces are extremely rare. No. 22 may, it is suggested, be a coin of Sardis; the form of the quadrate incuse being also similar.

82 Seleuceia in Syria. Tetradrachm, perhaps of Bosporic scale.

The type of the thunderbolt on a table refers to a legend that Seleucus Nicator was guided by lightning to the site of his new city. See Leake, *N. H.* For the scale, see n. 53.

83 Selge in Pisidia. Persian didrachm.

This coin much resembles another of Aspendus (no. 9).

84 Side in Pamphylia. Tetradrachm.

There can be little doubt that this and other similar coins were struck by Amyntas, king of Galatia, who must consequently have been master of Pamphylia also. See Div. 1 n. 81.

85 Do. Silver coin with Palmyrene legend. Persian didrachm.

This coin appears to be adjusted to the Persian scale, being double the weight of the Aryandic. (Div. 1 n. 85.) The saucer in the hand of the sacrificing figure is the φιάλη ἀμφαλωτή, the base being clearly visible in its centre.

86 Sidon in Phœnicia. Tetradrachm of Ptolemaic (Lagid) scale.

The autonomy of Sidon dates b.c. 110, after the struggles and reconciliation of Antiochus IX. and Antiochus X. The present coin, therefore, dated AII or 81, was struck b.c. 29.

87 Do. of Elagabalus (a.d. 218—222).

The type of Astarte (Ashtaroth) occurs frequently under various forms on the coins of Tyre, Tripolis, and Sidon.

88 Smyrna in Ionia. Gold stater.

The authenticity of the original of this unique piece (in the Bibliothèque Nationale at Paris) has been doubted. It represents a statue of Nemesis dedicated by the Prytanes. The obverse represents, according to some, Cybele; according to others, the Amazon Smyrna.

89 Do. Tetradrachm of fine work.

The legend ΖΜΥΡΝΑΙΩΝ for ΣΜΥΡΝΑΙ-ΩΝ is frequent on the coins of Smyrna.

90 Do. Do., without the lion on reverse, very fine work.

91, 92 Do. Small copper coins. *Obv.* OMHPOC. Homer seated, holding a staff in one hand and a book in the other. *Rev.* CMΥΡ-ΝΑΙΩΝ in wreath.

Coins of Colophon and Chios have likewise representations of Homer similar to the present. Salamis, Rhodes, Argus and Athens also claimed

Homer as their own; of which however, it is believed, their coins shew no signs. His head is represented on coins of Ios (one of the Cyclades), where he was said to be buried, and of Amastris in Paphlagonia, for some unknown reason; see Div. v. n. 81.

93 Do. of Severus Alexander (A.D. 222—235). First brass coin. *Obv.* A. K. M. CE. AAEEANAPOC., Head of Sev. Alexander to right. *Rev.* CMTPNAIΩN IIPΩTΩN ACIAC Γ. NEΩK. TΩN CEB. EII. C. IIOAEI-TOT, Heads of Sev. Alexander and his mother Julia Mamæa opposed; the former radiated (as the Sun), the latter with crescent behind (as the Moon).

The Ephesians, no less than the Smyrnæans, styled themselves "primates of Asia" (πρῶτοι Ἀσίας) on coins (Eck. D. N. V. ii. 517); and were also, as the Smyrnæans here boast of being, "thrice temple-wardens of the emperors." (γ. νεωκόροι τῶν Σεβαστῶν.) See remarks on n. 32.

94 Do. of Gordian III. (A.D. 238—244). Do. *Obv.* ATT. KAI. M. ANT. ΓΟΡΔΙΑΝΟC. His head to right. *Rev.* CMTPNAIΩN Γ. NEΩ. EII. TEPTIOT ACIAPXOT. Alexander's dream.

Alexander, hunting on Mount Pagus, lay down tired under a plane-tree near a temple of the Nemeses, who admonished him in a dream to found a city there, and bring the Smyrnæans thither. Apollo Clarius having confirmed their advice, the Smyrnæans migrated to Mount Pagus. (Eck. ii. 548.)

95 Do. Large brass coin.

The bust on the obverse is Ceres, or as some think Tranquillina (wife of Gordian III.), in the character of Ceres. The name of Tertius the Asiarch on the reverse shews that it belongs to her time. See n. 94.

The Asiarchs are mentioned in Acts xix. 31 ("chief of Asia," E. V.), and their office is the subject of a paper in the *Numismatic Chronicle* for 1860, by the author of this catalogue.

96 Tarsus in Cilicia. Didrachm of Persian scale (double siclos), struck by the satrap Absohar. *Obv. Baal Tars* (in Phœnician letters.) Jupiter of Tarsus sitting. *Rev.* Phœnician legend (" *This lion money was struck by Absohar, prince of Lower Cilicia*".) Lion and bull; building with towers below.

97 Do. Same denomination, without legend.

The Jupiter of this coin seems to be Baal Tars, whence the appropriation.

98 Do. Small silver medallion of Hadrian (A.D. 117—138).

The abbreviated legend of the obverse is in full : Αὐτοκράτωρ Καίσαρος Θεοῦ Τραϊανοῦ Παρθικοῦ υἱός, Θεοῦ Νέρβα υἱωνός, Τραϊανὸς Ἀδριανὸς Σεβαστός. The type of the reverse is thought by Leake to be Mithras, an oriental divinity. The original of this curious coin is in the collection of the Duc de Luynes.

99 Do. Autonomous copper coin.

The reverse is usually considered (but not by Leake) to be the tomb of Sardanapalus, who boasted of having founded Tarsus and Anchialo in one day. (See Div. i. n. 49.) The figure on one of its sides is evidently the same as n. 98. Leake thinks it is a small pyramidal temple or shrine.

100 Do. Copper coin of smaller size.

Same types, but the side of the structure differently ornamented (possibly a different side).

101 Do. of Gordian III. First brass coin.

Mithras, when cutting a bull's throat, as here, is more usually represented without rays, and in a Phrygian cap. The letters A.M.K. have been supposed to stand for ἀρίστη (sc. μητρόπολις), μεγίστη Κιλικίας. (Eck. iii. 77); Γ.Β. is for γράμματι βουλῆς = S.C. on Roman coins.

102 Teos in Ionia. Primitive silver coin; didrachm of Eginetan scale.

103 Do. Hemidrachm of Bosporic scale.

The cantharus, or cup of Bacchus, on the reverse of this coin, is precisely of the fictile form, which is most commonly found in Italy.

104 Tralles in Lydia. Cistophorus. (See n. 27.)

105 Tripolis in Phenicia. Tetradrachm of Greco-Asiatic scale.

M. Antony and Cleopatra are here represented with stars above, as the Dioscuri, the favourite deities of Tripolis. The date 31, of the Pompeian era = B.C. 33, when Antony and Cleopatra were exhibiting themselves at Alexandria, as Osiris and Isis. (See Div. I. nos. 103—107.) On the reverse is Astarte standing. The Pompeian era begins B.C. 64, when Pompey vanquished Tigranes and made all Syria free.

106 Do. of Caracalla (A.D. 211—217). Middle brass. The temple of Jove is on the right; that of Astarte on the left.

107 Do. of Elagabalus (A.D. 218—222). Do.

The temple on this coin, and one of the two temples on the preceding, have the symbol of Astarte in the pediment (compare n. 87); statues of Apollo and Diana occur in both. The architectural details on this and the preceding are in an unusually fine state of preservation.

108 Do. of Diadumenian (A.D. 217).

The date ΘΚΨ is of the Seleucid era, and = A.D. 217. The details of the ship are most beautifully preserved; the circular object near the mast-head is the carchesium, a term also applied to a vase of a somewhat similar form.

The boy-emperor Diadumenian, son of Macrinus, was murdered the same year that he was proclaimed Cæsar; his coins are consequently not very common. His portrait is of better execution than is usual on Greek imperial coins.

109 Tyre in Phenicia. Tetradrachm.

The temple of Hercules at Tyre was famous, to whom the types on both sides refer. The eagle on the prow occurs also on coins of Sidon (no. 86), and is probably adopted from

coins of the Ptolemies, the prow being very naturally substituted for the thunderbolt, and the palm added, as well as the club of Hercules.

The date 7 is of the Tyrian era, when Demetrius II. was slain at Tyre and the city became free, B.C. 126. This coin was therefore struck B.C. 119. The scale seems to be Ptolemaic; or, as Queipo calls it, Lagid.

110 Zeugma in Commagene, of Philip Senior (A.D. 244—249). Middle brass.

The town derived its name from its site near a bridge over the Euphrates. The temple on the reverse is on the summit of a mountain, and can be reached by two flights of steps, which are connected by a portico or passage below.

DIVISION III.

Continental Europe, excluding Italy.

1 Abdera in Thrace. Tetradrachm of Bosporic scale.

The gryphon is the type of Teos in Ionia, who peopled Abdera B.C. 544 (see Div. II. n. 102); hence also the Ionic form ΑΒΔΗΡΙΤΕΩΝ.

2 Acanthus in Macedonia. Attic drachm, apparently.

3 Do. Smaller silver coin, probably a tetrobolus.

The weights of the coins of Acanthus are perplexing. Leake obtained several of them on the site of Acanthus. These have no legends, and are of an early period; the former is nearly the weight of an Attic drachma, and the latter of an Eginetan hemidrachm, or Attic tetrobolus.

4 Acarnia. Olympic didrachm. *Obv.* Beardless human head of the river Achelous, with neck and horns of a bull; behind, ΑΤΚΟΤΡΙΟΣ. *Rev.* ΑΚΑΡΝΑΝΩΝ and monogram. Apollo seated, a bow in his hand.

The Lycurgus of the obverse of this beautiful coin is probably a magistrate; possibly, however, the artist. Magistrate's names are usually on the reverses of coins. See Div. I. n. 26. The drachma of Queipo's Olympic scale weighs 73,29 Troy grains; this scale may por-haps be regarded as a later and degraded form of what is called in this catalogue the Eginetan scale (i.e. the Commercial Attic of Queipo and Poole).

5 Achæan League *in genere*. Hemidrachm of the Eginetan scale.

The obverse of all the silver coins of the League has the head of Zeus Homagyrius, and the reverse has AX in monogram. The present coin has no additional letters on the reverse; but various cities of the League append their own initial letters or symbols, to which a magistrate's name (in whole or part) is often added; thus ΓΑ on the following is for ΓΑΛΕΙΩΝ, i.e. Elis. See nos. 61—64. For the scale, see Mr Finlay's remarks in *Num. Chron.* for 1866, p. 21.

6 Elis, struck for the Achæan League. Do.

7 Phlius, struck for the Achæan League. Copper coin.

The type of all the copper coins of the League is Jupiter Nicephorus; that of the reverse Juno. The copper coins bear the names of the various cities of the League at length, and usually some magistrate also.

8, 9 Ænus in Thrace. Tetradrachms, of fine old work, but light.

10, 11 Ætolia *in genere*. Tetradrachms. Slightly varied.

The type of the reverse (which has been variously explained,) is probably in both cases Ætolia personified, sitting on Macedonian armour; and the coin was most likely struck to commemorate the share which Ætolia (allied with Rome) took in vanquishing Philip V. and his Macedonians at the battle of Cynoscephalæ, B.C. 197.

12 Amphipolis in Thrace. Tetradrachm of very fine work, of the Bosporic scale.

The old Attic or Ionic form of the legend (ΑΜΦΙΠΟΛΙΤΕΩΝ) is explained by Amphipolis being a colony from Athens. See Leake, *N. H.* (Europe), p. 10.

13 Apollonia in Illyricum. Drachma.

The types (Cow and calf, and the gardens of Alcinous, so-called) are those of Corcyra, of which Apollonia was a colony; Dyrrhachium, another colony of Corcyra, has also the same types. See no. 39, and Div. v. no. 17. The coins of Apollonia have mostly the name of a magistrate in the nominative on one side, and another in the genitive on the other, where *fvi* seems to be understood. The latter is conjectured to be the Archon Eponymus. The weights of the coins of this city vary so much, that the scale is uncertain; Queipo regards it as Greco-Asiatic.

14 Do. Do. *Obv.* ΑΓΩΝΙΠΠΟΤ. Head of Apollo to left. *Rev.* ΑΠΟΛ across the field; ΔΙΝΟΚΡΑΤΗΣ ΕΡΙΜΝΑΣΤΟΤ in the exergue; three nymphs dancing round a hill from which fire issues, *i.e.* the Nymphæum, near Apollonia, mentioned by Strabo, a burning hill sacred to Pan and the Nymphs.

15 Argos in Argolis. Hemidrachm. (Eginetan scale). *Obv.* Fore part of wolf. *Rev.* A in quadrato incuse; a dot below it.

16 Athens. Gold stater, probably about the age of Alexander.

Down to the times of the orators Darics and Cyzicene staters seem to have been the gold currency at Athens.

19—23 Do. Tetradrachms of the same types, but of different periods.

The Athenian tetradrachm, held in the highest esteem for its purity, was the silver coinage of the old world in Greek times, and there exist barbarous imitations and forgeries.

The types of the tetradrachms of the early periods, reaching probably as late as Alexander, are always the head of Minerva on one side and her owl on the other, together with a sprig of olive (as well as a crescent on the later coins); the legend being invariably ΑΘΕ; this legend was retained on the much later tetradrachms from a conservative feeling, long after the Π had come into use; as especially n. 26, which bears the names of Micion and Eurycleides, demagogues of Athens B.C. 216, whom Philip V. put to death. Nos. 19—21 are probably much

earlier than the Persian wars. The style of nos.
22 and 23 prevailed during the 5th and 4th
centuries B.C.

24 Do. Decadrachm, same types.

Only two or three specimens of this coin
appear to be known; they seem to be rather
older (Leake thinks 'much older') than the
Persian wars. One in the British Museum has
a deep notch, which Leake calls 'the Persian
countermark'; it often occurs on coins of the
Persian empire, see Div. II. n. 96.

**25, 26 Do. Later tetradrachms with
magistrates' names, and of lighter
weight.**

The head of Pallas on this class of tetradrachms is quite different from the foregoing,
and is undoubtedly copied from her statue by
Phidias in the Parthenon. The secondary
symbols (caduceus on n. 25, and youths on
n. 26) are certainly connected in some way
with one of the magistrates. The date of n. 26
is about 216 B.C. See preceding remarks.

**27 Do. Later tetradrachm with mono-
grams of magistrates.**

28 Do. Drachms of the usual types.

The types are the same as the tetradrachm:
compare especially nos. 22, 23. The drachma,
whose normal weight was 67,5 grains, according to Leake, is very nearly the value of the
modern franc: it contains 6 obols, of 11,25
grains each. All the coins of Athens, certainly
known to be such, are of the scale of Solon;
and his reform seems to have consisted in re-
ducing the Eginetan standard to his new Attic
scale.

The reader (and especially the classical stu-
dent) is recommended to consult Leake's *Num.
Hell.* Europe, pp. 21, 22, for many valuable remarks both on the weights and history of the
coins of Athens, which are much too long for
insertion here. Since his death M. Beulé has
written an excellent work on them exclusively,
entitled *Monnaies d'Athènes*, Paris 1858, 4to,
with figures of all the principal forms in all
metals. Queipo estimates the Attic drachma
at 65,67 grains. In later times it was much
reduced and was at length considered equivalent to the Roman imperial denarius, which
weighed about 60 grains, varying at different
times.

29 Do. Triobol or hemidrachm.

The types and legend as on the earlier
tetradrachms, but the owl is seen in front and
is wingless. There are two olive-sprigs and no
crescent.

**30 Do. Trihemiobol, or obol-and-a-
half.**

Same types and legend as before, but the
owl has spread wings.

31 Do. Diobolus, or two-obol piece.

Same types and legend, but the owl has
two bodies and one head.

32 Do. Obols.

Same legend and types exactly as the
ordinary drachm and tetradrachm.

**33 Do. Half-obols, with precisely the
same types and legend.**

**34 Do. Tritemorion, or three-quarter
obol.**

Obverse as before, but AΘE and three
crescents on the reverse.

35 Do. Tartemorion, or quarter obol.

The same, but with one crescent only.
The number of crescents shews the number
of quarters of the obol.

**36 Do. Early copper coin, perhaps a
chalcus.**

Same types and legend; Minerva's head in
old style (n. 22), beside her an oil jar (amphora)
standing. This is among the earlier Athenian
pieces of copper (none of which can be older
than B.C. 406, when copper money was first
introduced), and may probably be about the
age of Philip. See Beulé, pp. 73—75. The
denominations of the copper money are difficult
if not impossible to determine.

37 Do. Late copper coin.

It is remarkable that no imperial Greek
copper coins (i.e. having an emperor's head)
of Athens exist. The present piece, however,
may (with Beulé) be referred to the imperial
period, the legend AΘHI indicating a very late
date. The design (Theseus killing the Minotaur)
varies a good deal on different Athenian coins.
Beulé, p. 398.

38 Do. Late copper coin.

The reverse of this excessively rare coin has AΘHNAIΩN, a sure proof of a late date (perhaps about the second century after Christ); it represents the theatre of Dionysus with one diazoma or concentric circular passage; above this are caverns in the rock, higher up the wall of the Acropolis, above which the Parthenon, and to the left of this the Propylæa. See Leake, *N. H.* p. 28, and Boulé, p. 394.

39 Do. Late copper coin, also reading AΘHNAIΩN (nearly effaced).

The contour of Neptune (not Jupiter, as Leake has accidentally written on the ticket) with Minerva for the possession of Attica occurs on the Parthenon (west front), on gems, and on vases. For this particular representation, taken from Athenian statues found near the Parthenon, fragments of which still remain, see Boulé, p. 393.

40 Do. Do.

The stairs seen on the right-hand side of the coin lead up to the Propylæa; to the left of which stands the Acropolis, the colossal figure of Minerva Promachus (conspicuous from afar to sailors) standing between them. The grotto of Pan is seen in the rock of the Acropolis (the actual statue of Pan included in it is now in this Museum); and above this the wall of the Acropolis, in which there is also a cavern.

This coin is very rare, and perhaps more in good preservation. See Leake, u. s. p. 28, and Boulé, p. 394.

41 Uninscribed silver coin (drachma), usually assigned to Athens. *Obv.* Half-horse (the hind quarters) to right. *Rev.* Quadrato incuse.

From Leake's miscellaneous cabinet, which is not included in his *Numismata Hellenica*. See Div. II. n. 1. For the reasons for attributing coins of this type to Athens, see Boulé, pp. 15—20. The *whole* horse also occurs as a *didrachm*. Similarly on other coins (e.g. Syracuse) the half of a type indicates *half* the value of the coin which has the *whole* type. The age of this coin can hardly be much later than Solon's Archonship (B.C. 594), to whose new Attic scale this class of money certainly belongs.

42 Bizye in Thrace of Caracalla (A.D. 211—217). Large brass.

The representations of the city-gates on different coins of Bizye differ rather considerably, and seem to indicate that architectural details have not been strictly adhered to in all cases. See Donaldson's *Archit. Numism.* nos. 83, 84.

43 Bœotia *in genere*. Archaic didrachm of the Eginetan scale.

44 Do. Similar didrachm of a good period of art. *Obv.* Bœotian shield. *Rev.* ETAPA (name of a magistrate, probably a Bœotarch); a crater (Bacchic vase); club (of Hercules) and grapes above.

The digamma may be noted in the legend. These Bœotian coins were probably struck at Thebes. See Leake.

45 Chalcidenses in Macedonia. Tetradrachm, Bœoric scale.

The city at which this beautiful piece was struck was probably Apollonia in Chalcidice, to which the types of Apollo and the lyre naturally point. See Leake, *N. H.* p. 33.

46 Do. Smaller silver coin, tetrobol, (same scale) with the same types.

47 Chersonesus of Thrace. Early didrachm (of the Eginetan scale).

Quidam prefers to regard this as a Græco-Asiatic tetradrachm.

48 Do. Later hemidrachms of the same scale, but lighter.

The pointed amphora or wine jar on this coin may be noted. Similar vessels were made down to Roman times, and a specimen found in this country is in this Museum. See also a representation of one (stuck in the ground) in a black-figure vase in Leake's collection.

49 Cleonæ in Argolis. Hemidrachm (Eginetan scale) of fine work.

50 Corinth. Primitive coin, didrachm. *Obv.* Pegasus with curled wings to left, below it the Koppa or ancient form of the letter K, (initial letter of Corinth). *Rev.*

4

Quadrate incuse of unusual form (peculiar to Corinth?).

This is the Corinthian stater divided into ten litræ; it is equivalent to the Attic didrachm.

51   Do.   Early coin (though later) of the same denomination.   *Obv.* Head of Pallas in Corinthian helmet to left, in sunk square.   *Rev.* Pegasus (bridled) to right, and Koppa.

52, 53   Do.   Later coins of the same denomination.

Types as before, but the Pegasus has pointed wings and no bridle. The obverses of these most beautiful and very common coins have various adjuncts (as a Hermaic statue on n. 52, a cock on a club n. 53, and very many others, see Leake); they probably are connected with the magistrates in whose time they were struck. The retention of the archaic koppa on those later coins (about the time of Alexander and later) may be compared with the retention of E for H on later coins of Athens. See n. 26. Leake thinks that the Corinthian standard was nearly the same as at Athens, or about 67 grains to the drachma.

54   Do. of Lucius Verus.   (A.D. 161—169).   Middle brass.

The imperial coins of Corinth are extremely numerous, and the legends are always in Latin, as is most generally the case when a Greek city was superseded by a Latin colony. The full legend of the reverse is COLONIA LAUS JULIA CORINTHUS, Julius Cæsar having colonised Corinth B.C. 46. The imperial coins very generally (as here, where Bellerophon mounted on Pegasus spears the Chimæra,) preserve the ancient traditions of their respective cities.

55   Cosa in Thrace.   Gold didrachm or stater.

Obtained by Col. Leake in Macedonia, where these coins are not very rare; who says "they were coined probably by order of M. Junius Brutus" (who is presumed to be represented between two lictors on the reverse) "when he commanded the Roman army in that country previously to the battle of Philippi." (B.C. 42).

56   Delphi in Phocis.   Diobolus, without legend, Eginetan scale.

The ram's head on the obverse is connected with the worship of Apollo or the Sun. The dolphins and Cretan goat's head of reverse may allude to Apollo having conducted Castalius from Crete to Delphi under the form of a dolphin. See Leake *N. H.* p. 45. Some coins with these types read ΔΑΑ or ΔΕΑ.

57   Do.   Obolus, also without legend, same scale.

The dot in the centre of the circle denotes that Delphi was the central point of the earth, (*umbilicus terræ*); while the tripod on the other side refers to the Delphic oracle of Apollo.

58   Do.   Copper coin of Hadrian.   (A.D. 117—138), reading ΔΕΛΦΩΝ.

For a somewhat different representation of Apollo Musagetes see Div. II. n. 52.

59   Dyrrhachium or Epidamnus in Illyricum.   Didrachm (of reduced Eginetan scale, apparently).

Types of the mother-city Corcyra. See Div. v. n. 17. The name Dyrrhachium alone (as here ΔΤΡ) occurs on the coins, none of which seem to be very early. Queipo considers the scale Persian.

60   Do. Didrachm of Attic scale, with Corinthian types on both sides. See n. 52.

Corcyra was a colony of Corinth; whence the Corinthian types of its daughter Dyrrhachium.

61—64   Elis regio.   Didrachms (of Eginetan scale) of fine old work.

The types of Jupiter and Juno, and in connexion with them of the eagle and thunderbolt, occur very generally on coins of Elis; the digamma of the legend (FA or FAΛEION) may be noted.

65   Epirus *in genere.*   Didrachm of Olympic scale.

The oak-wreath round the head of Jove indicates him to be the Jove of Dodona, where (as Leake thinks) the coins of Epirus were struck; the butting bull on the reverse probably symbolises the river Arachthus.

66   Do.   Drachma (same scale).   Monogram behind.   *Obv.* Head of

Jupiter Dodonæus to right, monogram behind. *Rev.* ΑΠΕΙΡΩΤΑΝ. Eagle on thunderbolt to right within oak-wreath.

67 Lacedæmon in Laconia, a tetradrachm (Attic scale?) struck by Cleomenes III. (B.C. 236—220). *Obv.* His portrait, with diadem, to left. *Rev.* Archaic statue of Apollo Amyclæus; in field ΛΛ (for ΛΑΚΕΔΑΙΜΟΝΙΩΝ) and a wreath.

Cleomenes III., who changed the Spartan form of government into a tyranny, is the only king who could have placed his portrait on coins of Lacedæmon or Sparta; the wreath indicates a victory, probably of Cleomenes III. over the Achæan League B.C. 225. For these matters and for the type of the reverse, see Leake, *N. H.* (Europe), pp. 55, 56.

The coin is evidently in imitation of the contemporary coins of the Seleucidæ, which accounts also for the Attic scale, adopted by Alexander and his successors in Syria. See Div. L nos. 41—43.

68 Do. Copper coin, struck in honour of their legislator Lycurgus.

The lunar C shews that the coin can hardly be very much anterior to the Christian era. (Compare late coins of Smyrna in honour of Homer. Div. II. n. 92.) The position of ΛΥ-ΚΟΥΡΓΟΣ on the obverse leaves little doubt that the head is not of Jove (as Eckhel half suspects, Vol. II. p. 280), accompanied by a magistrate's name, but that of the lawgiver himself. On many coins of Sparta we have the names of magistrates on the reverse.

69 Lamia in Thessaly. Hemidrachm (Eginetan scale). *Obv.* Ivy-crowned head of Bacchus to left, of beautiful work. *Rev.* ΛΑΜΙΕΩΝ. Crater, ivy-leaf above it; beside it an œnochoë.

The crater was the vessel holding the mixed wine and water, from which the liquor was drawn in the œnochoë or jug, and thence passed into the cylix (cup). See Vase-room, Div. III. and the model of the Campanian tomb.

70 Larissa in Thessaly. Eginetan didrachm of splendid work. *Obv.* Female head, full face, with frontlet, her hair hanging loosely in flowing tresses (the fountain Messeis? Hom. *Il.* x. 456). *Rev.* ΛΑΡΙΣΑΙΩΝ. Bridled horse to right.

The type of the obverse is undoubtedly a fountain personified (see a precisely similar coin of Syracuse, reading ΑΡΕΘΟΣΑ. Div. IV. n. 121), not Apollo, as Leake says. The type of the horse on this and the following coins may refer to the celebrity of the Thessalian horses (Leake); but it is more probably to be connected with the worship of Neptune. See no. 88.

71 Do. Drachma. *Obv.*, as before, but of inferior execution. *Rev.* ΛΑΡΙ. Horse feeding.

72, 73. Do. Drachmas, with other types.

For the *cuaria* or Macedonian hat seen on both coins see Div. L nos. 1. 2. The bull on n. 72 refers to the celebrity of Thessalian cattle. The female head on 73 may be the Nymph of the fountain.

74 Leto in Macedonia. Very early silver coin, didrachm of the Olympic scale.

For the scale see remarks on Div. L n. 1. This coin deserves attention as a very finely preserved specimen of the stiff and exaggerated style of the earliest art. This coin may be suspected to be about six centuries before Christ, more or less.

75, 76. Leucas in Acarnania. Didrachms with Corinthian types on both sides.

No. 75 has the less usual legend ΛΕΥΚΑ-ΔΙΩΝ; no. 76 has Λ only on both sides. Compare nos. 52, 53.

77, 78. Locri Ozolæ? Didrachms with Corinthian types.

Leake thinks that their coins were struck at Naupactus on the gulf of Corinth, the most important city of Locri Hesperii or Ozolæ,

4—2

The legends here are always, as it seems, ΛΟΚΡΩΝ or ΛΟΚΡ (to prevent confusion with Leucas?). It is however very doubtful whether these coins are not of the Locri Epizephyrii in S. Italy, on whose copper coins Corinthian types certainly occur (see Leake *N. H. Suppl.* p. 131); as appears by the annexed coin.

79 Locri Epizephyrii in S. Italy (out of its true place. See Div. iv. n. 29). Copper coin with Corinthian types.

For the coins of the Locrians of Opus see nos. 94, 95.

80 Macedonia. Gold medal, of third century A.D.?

Obtained by Col. Leake in Macedonia, and considered by him to have been probably struck to gratify Caracalla when passing through Macedonia (A.D. 214), who was a passionate admirer and imitator of Alexander. Both work and letters indicate a late date. None however regard the medal (for coin it can hardly be called) as a modern fabrication altogether.

81 Macedonia Prima, under the Romans. Tetradrachm.

L. Æmilius Paullus (B.C. 168) divided Macedonia into four provinces, a division which lasted about 20 years. Coins of the first, second, and fourth regions are known. The capital of ΜΑΚΕΔΟΝΩΝ ΠΡΩΤΗΣ was Amphipolis, where this coin was no doubt struck.

82 Macedonia under the Romans. Do.

Later than the preceding, when the four provinces were merged in one, with a bilingual inscription. *Obv.* ΜΑΚΕΔΟΝΩΝ. Head of Alexander, with ram's horn (compare Div. i. nos. 20, 21, 33 to right; behind, 84, (perhaps for Thessalonica). *Rev.* AESILLAS Q. (i.e. Quaestor. Cista of Bacchus, Club of Hercules, and Quaestor's Table; all within wreath.

83 Do. of late imperial period. Copper coin.

This portrait of Alexander is inscribed with his name, ΑΛΕΞΑΝΔΡΟΥ, in late letters. For the legend of the reverse KOINON MA-ΚΕΔΟΝΩΝ ΔΙC ΝΕΩΚΟΡΩΝ, see Div. ii. n. 10, and n. 32. No Neokor coins of Macedon are older than Caracalla.

84 Mantinea in Arcadia. Probably three-quarter obol-piece (τριτημόριον) of Eginetan scale. *Obv.* MAN (in archaic characters) between three acorns disposed like a tribolium, their stalks touching. *Rev.* Three taus similarly disposed. Compare no. 110.

The acorn alludes to the oak forests of Arcadia. Silver coins of Mantinea are very rare, contrary to what we should expect from so illustrious a city.

85 Maronea in Thrace. Very early uninscribed didrachm (of Eginetan scale).

The large and small incuse of the same type on the reverse are very peculiar. Coins of the same general types as the present read ΜΑΡΩ.

86 Do. Light (Attic) tetradrachm of a later period, of good work.

The cantharus above the horse (as well as the vine of the reverse) is a symbol of Bacchus, the tutelary god of Maronea; some of its coins read ΔΙΟΝΥΣΟΥ ΣΩΤΗΡΟΣ ΜΑ-ΡΩΝΙΤΩΝ.

87 Massalia in Gaul (Marseilles). Apparently a tetrobolon (Attic).

A very usual size and weight of the silver coins of Massalia; none seem to be larger; and none to be very ancient.

88 Megalopolis in Arcadia. Triobol or hemidrachm (Eginetan scale).

The city was founded B.C. 370 by Epaminondas, was in a state of decline about B.C. 180, and extinct before Strabo's time. The coins are mostly of the same age, style and denomination as those of the Achaean league. Compare nos. 5, 6.

89 Messene in the Peloponnese. Didrachm (Eginetan) of very fine work.

90 Do. Tetradrachm (late Attic).

This very rare coin is interesting as reading

IΘΩM on the reverse; shewing the figure to be the statue of Jupiter Ithomatus at Mess-ne.

91 Neopolis (Neapolis, Acts xvi. 11) of Macedonia (formerly Datus). Very early silver coin,(uninscribed) (Attic didrachm)) *Obr.* Head of Gorgo, full face. *Rev.* Four indentations in a square form.

92 Do. Later coin, of fine work. (Attic diobol, or rather Corinthian dilitron.) *Obr.* Same type. *Rev.* NEOII. Head of Venus to right, hair rolled and corded.

It is difficult to see by what scale the coins of Neopolis are regulated; see the weights of those given in *N. H.* (Europe) p. 70. It would seem to be most probably Corinthian.

93 Œniadæ of Acarnania. Copper coin of fine work. For type of obverse see n. 4.

94, 95 Opus in Locris. Didrachms (Eginetan) of very fine work.

Precisely similar coins read ΛΟΚΡΩΝ instead of ΟΠΟΝΤΙΩΝ; both were struck doubtless at Opus of the Locrians. Queipo is disposed to regard them as light Attic tridrachms.

96, 97. Orescii, in Thrace. Very early silver coins, of uncertain scale.

Both for weights and types of these coins compare Div. L n. 1, and Div. III. n. 72 respectively. They can hardly be much later than B.C. 500, to judge by the fabric, and yet contrary to expectation Η and Ω occur in the legends. For the Orescii, a tribe who probably lived among the Pangæan mountains, see Leake *N. H.* (Europe) p. 81.

98. Ortho in Thessaly. Copper coin.

The horse emerging from a woody rocky cavern alludes to the creation of that animal by a blow of Neptune's trident on a Thessalian rock, which was probably claimed for Ortho. See Leake, *Europ. Greece, Addend.* p. 162. This interesting and beautiful coin is thought to be unique.

99. Panticapæum of the Taurica. Gold stater (heavier than the Attic didrachm).

100. Do. Copper coin.

The Greeks connected Pan with Panticapæum, as appears by both these coins; Dr W. Smith thinks the name was probably Scythian. (Dict. Gongr. s, v.)

101 Phalanna in Thessalia. Drachma (later Eginetan) of beautiful work.

This is intermediate in weight between Queipo's Commercial Attic (Eginetan) and Olympic scales; and is one of several indications that there are varieties of one and the same Eginetan scale.

102 Pheneus in Arcadia. Didrachm (Eginetan) of very fine work.

On some coins of this type the name Arcas is written near the child. He was the son of Jove by Callisto, whom Mercury concealed from the jealous wrath of Juno.

103 Philippi in Macedonia (formerly Crenides). Gold stater (Attic didrachm).

One of the very few cities in Greece proper which struck gold; Philip IL discovered it in the neighbourhood, and named the city after himself. His and his son's (regal gold) coins were probably derived from the same mine.

104 Phlius in Achaia. Apparently a litra of the Corinthian scale.

There are coins of Phlius which have a whole butting bull on the obverse, which we should have expected would have been *double* the weight of the present coin, which has a *half* bull; in fact it is the *triple* of it, weighing about 40 grains, or three litræ. The scale of these coins can hardly be Eginetan; it seems rather to be Corinthian, which is perhaps not surprising, considering the proximity of Phlius to Corinth.

105, 106 Phocis *in genere.* Hemidrachms (Eginetan) of fine work.

The occurrence of Apollo's head on these coins leads to a suspicion that they were minted at Delphi, the principal city.

107 Platæa in Bœotia. Apparently a hemidrachm of the later Eginetan scale, (but light).

The head of Juno refers to her famous temple at Plataea, one of the most perfect in Greece in the time of Pausanias.

108 Sicyon in Achaia. Drachma (Eginetan).

The doves are sacred to Venus, who had a temple near Sicyon.

109, 110 Do. Didrachms, same scale.

The Chimaera (compounded of a lion, a goat, and a dragon) has reference to Bellerophon, "a hero not less honoured at Sicyon than at Corinth," Leake *N. H.* (Europe) p. 95, who gives reasons for attributing these coins to Sicyon. Cf. n. 34.

111 Do. Hemidrachm, same scale.

112 Stymphalus in Arcadia. Didrachm (Eginetan) of very fine work.

The Diana of the obverse had a temple at Stymphalus; on the reverse Hercules, whose lion's-skin is flying behind, is about to strike the Stymphalian birds, whom he has fairly put to flight from off this coin, though on other coins of Stymphalus they appear; sometimes with Hercules on one side and the bird on the other.

113 Thebes. Gold coin of fine early work, apparently a hemidrachm of the Eginetan scale. *Obv.* Head of Bacchus (ivy-crowned) to right. *Rev.* [Θ] E. The infant Hercules strangling the serpents (sent by Juno to destroy him). Weight 47 grains, size 2, (Mionnet's scale).

From Lord Northwick's collection, sold in 1859 after the publication of the *Num. Hell.*, and therefore not included therein. Thebes is very nearly, if not quite, the only city in Greece proper which struck gold before the time of Philip II., and these are of the highest rarity; there are a few gold coins of early looking fabric ascribed to Macedonia and Thrace, whose genuineness is somewhat doubtful. Even in Philip's time and long afterwards very little gold was struck by any city in Greece proper; gold coins of Philippi, Athens, and Ætolia in genere being excessively rare, and those of any other place (e.g. Chalcis in Macedonia) being

either unique or nearly so. The regal gold of Philip, Alexander, and Lysimachus is abundant.

114—118. Do. Various early silver coins adapted to the Eginetan scale; drachma (n. 114), obol (n. 115), didrachm (116, 117, 118).

The type of all on the obverse is the Boeotian shield, which occurs on various other Boeotian cities (e.g. Orchomenus, Plataea n. 107, Tanagra, Thespiae nos. 125, 126); the reverse of all have incuses of various forms. No. 114 has no letter; nos. 115, 116, 117 have Θ, only of different archaic forms; no. 118 has ΘΕΒΑ.

119 Do. Three quarter obol-piece, (τεταρτημόριον.) Of the same scale, (as also the two following).

The three half-shields correspond to the three crescents on the coins of Athens (n. 34) of the same denomination, but of a different scale: the normal weight of this coin being nearly 12 grains, that of Athens nearly 9. Compare no. 84.

120—123 Didrachms (later, but early and of good work).

On n. 120 and n. 123 the Θ is of the modern form, but the E is not replaced by Η, as on some later coins. For the crater on n. 123, compare n. 69.

124 Do. Hemidrachm.

The vase on this coin is a cantharus, the cup of Bacchus and his attendant route. See n. 84.

125 Thespiae in Boeotia. Obol (Eginetan) of early work.

The form of the sigma deserves notice.

126 Do. Didrachm (Eginetan) of fine work.

The legend ΘΕΣΠΙΚΟΝ is in regimen with the coin understood, whether νόμισμα (Leake) or δίδραγμον.

127, 128 Thessaly in genere. Drachms (Eginetan) of rather late work.

For the Pallas Itonia on these coins see Div. I. n. 23.

129 **Thessalonica in Macedonia. Copper coin of good work.**

The city was built by Cassander B.C. 315 or thereabouts, and this coin seems not very much later, to judge by the fabric. It is singular that all the coins of this city, the metropolis of *Macedonia secunda* so famous in profane and sacred history, should be of copper only; they are very numerous both autonomous and imperial. It is quite probable however that tetradrachms of the Roman period were struck there. See n. 52.

130 **Do. of Philip junior (A.D. 247—249).** *Obv.* MAP. IOTAIOC ΦIΛIΙΙΙOC AT [ΤOΚΡΑΤΩΡ.] His radiated bust to right. *Rev.* ΘECCAΛO-NIKEΩN NEΩKOP. A tripod; its caldron holding five (balloting?) balls.

Thessalonica is one of the very few Neokor cities in Europe; they are nearly all in Asia. Perinthus in Thrace is another instance, and the Macedonians generically are called Neokoroi. See n. 53.

131 **Thyrrheium in Acarnania. Silver coin of the same scale and types as n. 4, and half its value. (Olympic drachma.)**

We can hardly doubt that coins of Acarnania in genere were struck here.

132 **Do. Corinthian stater (= Attic didrachm) with Corinthian types.**

133 **Tyras in Sarmatia. Drachma (later Eginetan) of spirited work.**

This city was situated, according to Leake, on the Dniester about 15 or 20 miles from its mouth, and with Olbia was the most northern limit of Greek civilisation.

DIVISION IV.

EUROPE CONTINUED, ITALY AND SICILY.

§ 1. *Italy.*

The Greek cities of Italy and Sicily being in a great degree Achæan, their scale, as Leake remarks, appears to be mostly Corinthian; but the weights of the drachm and didrachm vary a good deal, as the following coins shew; and some probably belong to other scales. Some of the copper money are parts of the Roman as.

1 **The Brettii, or Bruttii. Gold drachm.**

Compare the coins of Pyrrhus (Div. I. n. 29). Both are probably nearly contemporary, and struck at Consentia, the chief city of the Brettii, a barbarous tribe who revolted from the Lucanians about B.C. 356, and were subdued by the Romans under L. Papirius Cursor (B.C. 274); but did not utterly disappear from history till after the close of the second Punic war, (about B.C. 200). They inhabited Calabria Citra and Calabria Ultra.

2, 3 **Do. Silver drachms (heavier than usual), of good work.**

The weights of the silver coins of the Brettii vary a good deal.

4 **Do. Copper coin.**

The types of this coin (Hercules and Pallas) are the same as on some coins of the Lucani. The coins of the Brettii seem to have been mostly struck a little before and after B.C. 300.

5 **Do. Do.** *Obv.* Head of Jove to right; ear of corn behind. *Rev.* ΒΡΕΤΤΙΩΝ. Eagle, crescent, and horn of plenty. Size 5.

6 **Do. Do.**

7 **Do. Do.**

8 **Do. Do.** *Obv.* Head of Victory to left. *Rev.* Jupiter fulminating in a biga to left; under horses grapes.

9 **Do. Do.** *Obv.* Same type, with NIKA. *Rev.* ΒΡΕΤΤΙΩΝ. Jupiter standing to right, fulminating; in field, star and horn of plenty.

The copper coins of the Bruttii are commonly well preserved, and sometimes (as these) in a very fine state. As a general rule Greek copper coins have suffered considerably from circulation or time or both; the quality of the metal is not the same in all cases, which may account for a good deal. When it is chemically changed into a green or blue varnish (as n. 4, n. 39 &c), the coin is said to be *patinated*.

10 **Cales in Campania. Didrachm of good work.** The Latin legend (CALENO) on all the coins of Cales shew that they belong to the Roman colony, B.C. 331.

11 **Caulonia in Bruttium. Very early didrachm of the Incuse type.** *Obv.* KAΥΛΟ. Nude youthful figure with long hair to right (Apollo?) holding a branch in his right hand, and a figure with winged heels, (Hermes?) in his left: in field, stag (symbol of Artemis, associated in worship with Apollo). *Rev.* Same legend and types but incuse (i.e. *in intaglio*).

The incuse coinage is peculiar to Magna Graecia: commonly the same type and legend (or nearly so) occur on both sides, (compare nos. 13, 30, 31, 43, 53, 56); but sometimes the incuse type is altogether different from that in relief (as no. 14, 32).

12 **Do. Later but early didrachm.**

Caulonia was founded from Achaia towards the end of the eighth century B.C. and depopulated by the elder Dionysius B.C. 388. The coin lies within these limits.

13 **Crotona in Bruttium. Early didrachm with tripod in relief and incuse.**

14 **Do. Do. but the incuse type of the reverse is an eagle.**

15 **Do. Do. but both types are in relief.**

The Koppa (whence the Latin Q) for Kappa shews these three coins to be early; it is the only example, it is believed, of this letter occurring on coins not *followed by the vowel O.* We have the letter on early coins of Syracuse (n. 115), Corcyra (Div. IV. n. 21), and Corinth (Div. III. nos. 50—53), where it is retained by an affected archaism on its late coins.

16—19 **Do. Later didrachms of beautiful work, the types referring to the worship of Juno, Apollo, and Hercules.**

From all these coins the old Koppa has disappeared. The obverse of n. 18 is the Lacinian Juno, whose temple was a few miles from Croton. The vessel held by Hercules on the reverse of the same coin is his own peculiar cup, the *scyphus* (see also n. 22). Several varieties of this cup may be seen in the Vase-collection (Periods I. II. III. IV.)

20, 21 **Cumæ in Campania. Early didrachms.** The female head on the obverse is uncertain, perhaps Parthenope (not the Cumæan Sibyl, of whom the earlier Greek authors know nothing); for another representation of Scylla (on n. 21) see n. 74.

22, 23 **Heraclea in Lucania. Didrachms of very fine work.**

Hercules (who occurs on the reverse of both coins, and indeed of most of the city) was also a favourite deity at Tarentum, from which Heraclea was colonised B.C. 432. "Some of the coins of Heraclea may deservedly be reckoned among the choicest specimens of Greek art." (Bunbury, in Smith's *Dict. Gr. and Rom. Geogr.* s. v.)

24—26 **Velia or Hyele in Lucania. Didrachms of beautiful work.**

The letters KΛΕΤΑΟΡΟΥ above the frontlet of Minerva (n. 25) are quite microscopic, (compare nos. 121, 132); Cleodorus was probably the artist.

27 **Hyrina (in Campania?) Didrachm of fine early work, with retrograde legend.**

The andromorphous bull of the reverse is said to be an exclusively Campanian type (occurring on coins of Neapolis and Nola, see nos. 38, 40), and has led numismatists to place this Hyrina in that province. The coins of Hyrina and Nola are sometimes found in company, which leads to a suspicion that the cities were not far apart. Hyrina in Campania is not mentioned by any ancient author whatever, and its existence is established by its coins alone.

28 Italian league for promoting the Social War (B.C. 90—88). Denarius of rather barbarous fabric with Oscan legend. *Obv.* Head of Bacchus to right; in front MVTIL. EMBPATVB.(*i.e.*Mutilus Imperator). *Rev.* Bull (symbol of Italian league) goring wolf (symbol of Rome): in exergue C. PAAPI (*i.e.* Calus Papius).

The coins of this league are thought to have been struck at Corfinium in Samnium. They chose consuls in imitation of Rome, Q. Pompedius Silo, and C. Papius Mutilus, both of whose names occur on coins. This coin, taking both its sides, reads (in Latin): C. Papius Mutilus, Imperator (*i.e.* consul).

29 Locri Epizephyrii in Bruttium. Didrachm. See Div. III. nos. 78, 79; one or both of which belong here.

30—32 Metapontum in Lucania. Early coins with incuse types.

The plant represented on all these coins is bearded wheat (not barley as Leake). The incuse type of nos. 30, 31 is a repetition of the obverse; but the reverse of n. 32 has a bull's head.

33—37 Do. Didrachms of beautiful work.

The head on 31 is that of Mars; on 33, 36, Ceres (of the most exquisite execution); on 37 Venus, apparently, but perhaps Ceres.

38 Neopolis in Campania (Naples). Didrachm.

The head of the obverse is probably Parthenope, the Siren, who gave her name to the place.

39 Do. Copper coin, beautifully patinated. *Obv.* NEOΠOΛITΩN. Head of Apollo to left; behind, T. *Rev.* Victory crowning human-headed bull; two letters (IΣ ι) below.

The andromorphous bull according to some symbolizes Bacchus; according to others the river Glanis.

40 Nola in Campania. Didrachm. (See remarks on n. 27.)

41 Nuceria Alfaterna in Campania. Didrachm. Type of the obverse (horned head) uncertain; Bacchus (Eckhel); the river Sarnus (Leake); Alexander the Great, according to others (Eckhel). See Div. I. nos. 20, 21.

The retrograde legend (in Oscan characters) is in Greek letters NTFKPINΩN AΛA-ΦATEPNΩN. Leake thinks the coins are of the third century B.C.

42 Populonium (Pupluna on coins) in Etruria. Double denarius (as denoted by LX).

The flat smooth reverse (without type or indentation) is peculiar, or very nearly so, to Populonia. Some early British coins have also a blank reverse, but it is very convex. See *Select. of Brit. Coins*, n. 5.

43 Poseidonia, afterwards Pæstum, in Lucania. Very early didrachm with same types on both sides (in relief and incuse).

Fine old work. The Sigma in this coin (which reads ΠOΣ) resembles M; the ancient Mu may be seen on n. 30, where the left-hand stroke is longest.

44 Do. Didrachm of a more recent period, good work.

45 Do. Copper coin, reading ΠAIS-TANO.

The name seems to have been corrupted into Pæstum about three centuries B.C. (more or less).

46 Do. Copper coin (a triens designated by the four globules). *Obv.* Head of Bacchus, four globules behind. *Rev.* ΠAIS. Horn of plenty and four globules: in field ear of branched corn (wheat).

Leake's conjecture that the plant is Maize is out of the question; the *Zea Mays* being a native of the West Indies, and consequently unknown in Europe before the discovery of America.

47 **Rhegium in Bruttium. Tetradrachm (heavy).**

Anaxilas of Messenian origin, because tyrant of Rhegium B.C. 494. Aristotle tells us that he introduced the hare into Sicily, and also won a chariot-race of mules at Olympia; and that he accordingly placed the hare and mule-chariot on the coins of Rhegium, the types of the present coin, which is probably of the age of Anaxilas. See coins of Messana below (Nos. 92—93), and the remarks.

48 Do. Do.; fine early work. *Obv.* Lion's head seen in front. *Rev.* PHΓINON. Head of Apollo. Two leaves of olive behind.

The lion's head is a Samian type, and is no doubt placed on the coins of Rhegium, because of the assistance which the Samians gave Anaxilas in conquering Zancle. See below, n. 92.

49 Do. Drachma (same types).

50 Do. Hemidrachm. *Obv.* Same type. *Rev.* PH, and sprig of olive.

51 Do. Copper coin of beautiful work.

52 **Uncertain of Campania.** Gold didrachm (or denarius). *Obv.* Head of Janus. *Rev.* ROMA. Kneeling figure holding a pig; a military chief standing on either side of him, touching the pig with a sword.

This is evidently an 'alliance' coin, probably between Rome and some city of Italy. *Cf.* Stahunt, et cum jungebant foedera porca. Æn. VIII. 641. Col. Leake considers coins reading ROMA or ROMANO to have been struck in Rome itself; others, as Mr Burgon, regard them as having been struck in various cities of Campania under Roman influence. The Romans first struck silver money B.C. 269.

53 Do., reading *Romano*. **Silver didrachm** (early denarius according to Leake).

The Romulus and Remus of the reverse may seem to favour the view that the coin was struck in Rome. The denarius, which at first weighed about 112 grains Troy, gradually fell, according to Leake, to about 60 grains in the

first century B.C. In imperial times it varied rather considerably.

54 **Suessa in Campania. Didrachm.** *Obv.* Head of Apollo to right. *Rev.* Naked man on a horse to left, a palm branch on his shoulder, by his side another bridled horse; in exergue SVESANO.

Leake considers that Suesano is for Suessano the old Latin genitive; on some Lucanian coins we have AOTKANOM. The present coin is probably of the second or third century B.C.

55 **Sybaris, afterwards Thurii, in Lucania.** Didrachm of the earliest work (incuse types).

56 Do. Drachma, same types.

Sybaris was founded about B.C. 720, and almost destroyed B.C. 510. "The extant coins, therefore, of Sybaris are of the sixth or seventh century B.C., and some of them are among the most ancient to be found either in Greece or Italy."—Leake, who considers the bull to symbolise the river Crathis. For the form of the Sigma in the legend (ΣT), see n. 43.

57—59 **Thurii. Tetradrachm** (n. 87), and didrachms (nos. 58, 59), of very fine work.

The figure on the helmet of Pallas is Scylla; see n. 74. The coins of Thurii are considered to be among the very finest ever struck by the Greeks.

60—62 **Tarentum in Calabria.** Gold didrachms of very beautiful work.

63 Do. Gold obol, or rather litra.

Aristotle mentions that on the coins of Tarentum, Taras, the son of Neptune, was represented riding on a dolphin. Tarentum is the only city in Magna Græcia which had a gold coinage of any considerable extent, all the coins, however, being rare.

64—67 Do. Didrachms of good work.

The silver didrachms of Tarentum are immensely numerous; in Carelli's work on the money of ancient Italy more than 300 varieties are figured.

68 **Temesa in Bruttium. Didrachm,** of early date.

Termre, a port to which Homer mentions that Greek ships went to obtain copper in exchange for iron, is identified by Strabo, Ovid, and Statius with the Temese or Tempsa in Magna Graecia. See Leake, p. 150.

69—72 Terina in Bruttium. Didrachms.

No. 71 is a very early coin, as appears both by the style of art, and by the forms of the letters; NIKA on the reverse, indicates the figure to be that of Victory. Nos. 69, 70 are also considerably ancient, as appears by the legend TEPINAION, which in the more recent coin n. 72, becomes TEPINAIΩN. The obverse of n. 71 (marked TEPINA), and the reverses of 70 and 72 (also marked TEPINA), are figures of Terina, the nymph of the fountain, which gave name to the city. The obverses of 69, 70, 72 are considered by Leake to represent the Siren Ligeia, sister of Parthenope (see n. 38), whose monument stood on the river Arve, near to which Terina stood.

§ 2. Sicily, and adjacent Islands.

(Scale mostly Attic, or rather Corinthian; see n. 111.)

73 Acragas, or Agrigentum (Girgenti). Tetradrachm.

The inscription is written boustrophedon, i.e. partly ascending, partly descending. The crab is the freshwater crab of the Mediterranean, which shews that the coin symbolises the river (not harbour) of Girgenti.

74 Do. Do., but much more spread.

The original of this most beautiful piece fetched at Lord Northwick's sale, £139.

75 Do. Decadrachm.

This denomination occurs also among coins of Syracuse. The original of this coin (at Paris) is believed to be unique.

76 Camarina. Tetradrachm of early work.

The microscopical letters on the plinth (EΞAKEΣTIΔAΣ) probably denote the artist. The vases in the exergue are amphorae. Compare Athens (Div. III. nos. 25—27) and Chios (Div. v. n. 12).

77 Catana. Tetradrachm of early work.

78 Do. Do., later; of fine but rather mannered execution.

79 Gela. Small gold coin. One and a half litra, apparently. (Lagid diobol, according to Queipo).

Sosipolis is an epithet of the Oukleus (Proserpine?) represented. Soteira occurs similarly on copper coins of Agathocles as an epithet of Diana.

80, 81 Do. Tetradrachms of fine early (n. 80) and later (n. 81) work.

82 Himera. Drachma (Eginetan), early work.

83 Do. Tetradrachm (Attic), of fine work.

The female holding a phiale or patern, the bust (epibolos) of which is visible, is probably the nymph of Himera (cf. n. 109, 110); and the companion faun (upon whom the hot water descends) symbolises the sufferers who derive benefit from the baths, or Thermae, as Himera was afterwards called.

84 Leontini. Tetradrachm of fine old work.

85 Do. Do.

86 Do. Didrachm.

87 Do. Obolus, or rather litra.

88 Lipara. Copper coin, reading ΛIΠAPAION.

The genitive ending in -ON is very unusual on copper coins; money in that metal being in almost all cases later than 400 B.C., and nearly all coins having the O for Ω in the genitive being of the fifth century B.C. or only a little earlier or later; coins much earlier than 500 B.C. having either abbreviated legends or none. The present coin seems to be about 400 B.C.; at any rate not much earlier.

89 Melita (Malta). Bilingual copper coin of the Roman period.

The sella curulis or Roman chair of state is

5—2

represented on this and on various Roman coins.
C. Arruntanus Balbus was doubtless propraetor
of Sicily, to which Malta belonged.

**90 Do. Copper coin with foreign
(Egyptian?) types, but Greek legend.**

The veiled head crowned with the lotus
may probably be Isis; the four-winged figure
Osiris.

**91 Messana (Messina), formerly Zan-
cle. Drachma (Eginetan scale).**

Zancle, here written Dank[le], is a Sicilian
word signifying a sickle; the sickle on this coin
symbolising the noble harbour of Messina, the
projections being perhaps buildings. This very
early coin may be safely ascribed to the sixth
century B.C. See below.

**92 Do. Tetradrachm (Attic scale);
or rather a double decalitron of
the Corinthian scale.**

Anaxilas, tyrant of Rhegium, by the help
of some Samians and Messenians (from the
Peloponnese) seized Zancle 494 B.C., and
changed its name to Messene. The types of
this coin (calf's and lion's head) are Samian,
and occur also on some coins of Rhegium.

The form of the legend and of the letters
indicate that this early and very rare coin is
contemporaneous with Anaxilas.

93 Do. Do.

The hare was introduced into Sicily by
Anaxilas, whence the type, as Aristotle tells us;
the same type on both sides occurs also on some
rare coins of Rhegium; see n. 47.

94 Do. Do., very fine work.

The legend now becomes MEΣΣANION
(Doric form), having previously been MEΣΣENI-
ON. The Doric dialect came in with Dionysius
I. tyrant of Syracuse, who in 396 B.C. took
Messene, and transported most of its population
to Tyndaris. The genitive ending in -ON
shews that this coin cannot be much later than
that event. The head accompanied by the
syrinx is probably that of Pan, though without
horns.

95 Do. Do., also of fine work.

Later than the preceding, and reading
MEΣΣANION (not MEΣΣANION).

**96 Do. Copper coin of very fine
work, bearing the name of the
Mamertini.**

About 282 B.C. some Oscan mercenaries
of Agathocles, tyrant of Syracuse, after his
death B.C. 289, treacherously seized Messina,
and massacred the inhabitants. They ruled
the city under the name of Mamertini, i.e. sons
of Mamers or Mars (the head of Mars and the
legend APEOΣ occur on this coin), and struck
coins bearing their name; which are of un-
commonly fine work, but all of copper. They
allied themselves with Rome and continued to
rule Messina till the reign of Augustus in their
own name. The coins of Messina from first
to last are amongst the most historical in the
whole Greek series.

**97 Naxos. Tetradrachm. Very fine
old work.**

The squatting faun on the reverse holds
a cantharus, the sacred drinking-cup of Bacchus,
whose head is on the obverse.

**98—105 Formerly classed to Panor-
mus, but now considered to belong
to Carthage. They have either no
legends or else Punic legends or
letters.**

**98 Stater of electrum, of the Egine-
tan scale (L. Müller *Numism. de
l'Afrique Anc.* vol. II. p. 185.
Copenh. 1860).**

The symbol above the horse on the reverse
is thus explained by Müller: "Le symbole égyp-
tien, composé d'un disque radié, flanqué de
deux serpents portant chacun un disque sur la
tête, nous présente le soleil combiné avec le
serpent aspic, qui par les égyptiens était appelé
oaro, urœus, et considéré comme symbole de la
divinité. Cet emblème est sans doute celui
d'Osiris, dieu du soleil." Id. p. 119. This coin
is his n. 64 of Carthage, p. 85, and as no Greek
coin is in this style of art, as regards the head
of Ceres, "elle doit être regardée comme pro-
prement carthaginoise."

99 Gold stater of the Olympic scale. Id. p. 134.

This very elegant coin, "où la beauté s'unit à la noblesse," is n. 45 of Carthage in Müller, pp. 81, 112.

100 Eighth part of the Olympic gold stater. Müller n. s. n. 79 (Carthage), p. 87.

101 Silver decadrachm of the Phenician (i.e. Bosporic) scale, according to Müller, p. 136.

This coin is his n. 127; the Phenician legend whose letters, rendered into Hebrew, are רשרא is considered to express "le nom de Byrsa, citadelle de Carthage." p. 123.

102 Tetradrachm, of the Attic scale, struck by Carthage in Sicily, according to Müller, p. 75. *Obv.* Head of Ceres with blades of wheat in her hair to left, surrounded by four dolphins. *Rev.* Bust of horse, Punic legend (*Am-machanat, i.e. people of the camp*) below. Müller n. 18 (Carthage).

The interpretation of the legend is uncertain: some understand Panormus to be intended by it, others Carthage itself.

103 Do., according to Müller. *Obv.* Head of Hercules. *Rev.* Bust of horse and palm-tree. Legend as before. Müller n. 8 (Carthage).

104 Do., to judge by the weight. *Obv.* Head of Ceres with dolphins. *Rev.* Quadriga and Punic legend below.

This is apparently not included in Müller's work. The types on both sides are those of Syracuse.

105 Do., according to Müller. *Obv.* half horse crowned by victory, in field grain of barley: below Punic legend *Kart-chadasat (i.e. new

town). *Rev.* Palm; and Punic legend *Machanat (i.e. camp)* as before.

Müller n. 3 (Carthage).

106 Segesta. Didrachm of fine work.

107 Do. Tetradrachm of very fine early work.

The figure of a hunter in a Phrygian cap is considered to be Acestes, a Trojan, and the mythical founder of Segesta.

108 Selinus. Early didrachm (but heavy).

109 Do. Tetradrachm of fine old work (light).

110 Do. Didrachm (light).

The Selinuntians suffered from a plague, arising from the marshy character of their soil; the philosopher Empedocles of Agrigentum (who flourished 444 B.C.) recommended works of drainage, and so the pestilence ceased. The types of the river-gods Hypsas and Selinus sacrificing at the altar of Aesclepius (which bears his symbol a cock) have reference, as is generally thought, to this happy event (nos. 109, 110).

The Apollo and Diana of n. 109, are the deities who can shoot or withhold their plague-bearing arrows. Selinus was destroyed or nearly so about 409 B.C., and all its coins appear to be of the fifth and sixth centuries B.C.

111—148 Syracuse and Tyrants of Syracuse.

The coins of Syracuse are amongst the most beautiful of the whole Greek series, and are also exceedingly numerous, ranging from the sixth century B.C. to the reign of Hieronymus the last tyrant, who died 215 B.C., and perhaps later. The city was taken by Marcellus 212 B.C.; but its power of striking money may have been retained, as it became a most favourite resort with its Roman masters. The monetary scale of Syracuse is the same as that of Corinth the mother city; the litra, weighing about 13 grains, being the unit. As the Corinthian stater of 10 litra was nearly equivalent to the Attic didrachm, it is common to render the Syracusan money into Attic denominations.

111   Gold piece of eight litræ, apparently. Extremely fine work.

112   Gold litra.

The same unit of measure, having nearly the same types, occurs also in silver. n. 120.

113   Gold drachma (*i. e.* five litræ).

The head on this and the following coin is that of Apollo, and is so described by Leake himself in the *Numismata Hellenica*. The triscelium, or triquetra, which is found on various coins of Asia, as well as of Sicily, is probably a religious emblem. It is now the arms of the Isle of Man.

114   Gold drachma, of fine work. *Obv.* Head of Apollo to the left; behind, star. *Rev.* ΣΤΡΑΚΟΣΙΩΝ. Tripod.

None of the gold coins of Syracuse seem to be earlier than the Dionysii; the earliest appear to be those of Evænetus and Cimon. (*Trans. Royal Soc. Lit.* for 1850, p. 301.)

115   Very early silver tetradrachm, probably about 500 B.C. or a little later.

The style indicates a very remote antiquity.

116   Very early silver didrachm, but later than the preceding; probably about 500 B.C.

This coin, alone of all here exhibited, has the Koppa (ϙ) in place of the Kappa (K) in the legend; and may safely on that account be regarded as earlier than any of them. See n. 128.

117, 118   Early silver tetradrachms, probably of the earlier part of the fifth century B.C.

119   Early silver tetradrachm, probably of the latter part of the fifth century B.C.

The penultimate letter of the last four coins being O not Ω shews that none of them can be placed later than about 400 B.C. The archonship of Euclid, when the long vowels were first used in public documents, is 403 B.C.;

but it is certain that in more places the short vowels survived a few years later. See n. 94.

120   Silver litra, early work. *Obv.* Female head (Proserpine) to right; in front ΣΤΡΑ. *Rev.* Sepia.

The litra was a little heavier than the Attic obol; the former is estimated by Leake to weigh 13.5 Troy grains, the latter 11.25 grains.

121   Later tetradrachm of magnificent work by Cimon; of the middle of the fourth century B.C.

The head represents the fountain of Arethusa, and the word ΑΡΕΘΟΣΑ in small letters may still be read; this orthography indicates the coin to be early; in the Macedonian series OT first takes the place of O in the genitive in the reign of Philip II. 359—336 B.C. On the frontlet the word ΚΙΜΙΝ occurs in microscopic letters, Cimon being doubtless the artist (*see* n. 132); the occurrence of the Ω indicating that the coin could not be earlier than about 400 B.C. Taking all circumstances into account we may place its date about 350 B.C. more or less, or in the reign of Dionysius II. (367—343 B.C.).

122   Later tetradrachm, shewing the horses of the quadriga in extreme action.

The full legend is not visible on this specimen; the penultimate letter was Ω. See Combe Hunt. Mus. tab. 52. f. 15.

123   Another in a different style.

124   Rather early silver tetradrachm of most elaborate execution, by Euclid, whose name (ΕΥΚΛΕΙΔ) may be traced in microscopical letters on the helmet of Pallas. Probably about 400 B.C.

On another tetradrachm this artist's name occurs where the legend is not as here ΣΤΡΑΚΟΣΙΟΣ (understand ΝΟΤΜΜΟΣ), but ΣΤΡΑΚΟΣΙΟΝ, so that the coin cannot be much later than 400 B.C.; and the exceedingly elaborate and delicate treatment indicates that it cannot be much earlier.

125 Silver hemidrachm.

126 Silver didrachm, with Corinthian types on both sides, in a later style of art.

Syracuse was colonised from Corinth about 734 B. C., and like many other Corinthian colonies sometimes adopted the types of the mother-city.

127 Apparently a silver piece of twelve litræ; in a later style of art.

The Diana Venatrix is probably a copy of an ancient statue.

128 Silver decadrachm, or pente-contalitron; Queen Demarete's piece.

The date of this magnificent coin is known within a year, having been struck by Gelon I. after concluding a peace with Carthage 480 B. C. As he died 478 B. C., we may place this coin 479 B. C. The proceeds of a present made by the Carthaginians to his wife Demarete furnished the metal for these coins; νόμισμα ἐξέκοψε τὸ κληθὲν ἀπ' ἐκείνης Δαμαρέτειον τοῦτο δ' εἶχεν Ἀττικὰς δραχμὰς δέκα· ἐκλήθη δὲ παρὰ τοῖς Σικελιώταις ἀπὸ τοῦ σταθμοῦ πεντηκοντάλιτρον (Diod. Sic. XI. 26).

It will be observed that although the Ω does not occur in the legend, the ordinary K does; so that all coins of Syracuse which have a Koppa in the legend (see n. 116) may safely be pronounced earlier than 480 B. C. The style of this coin enables to date approximately others which approach it; e. g. nos. 117, 118.

129 Ditto. Decadrachm, often called the Syracusan medallion.

Below the lowest dolphin of the obverse are traces of ETAINETO, the artist's name, (Evenetus) in the old genitive. In the exergue of the reverse are seen a shield, a cuirass, greaves, and a helmet; below them in some specimens (as in 130) may be read ΑΘΛΑ (*the prize*) in very small letters. They were the reward of the victor in the chariot-race.

130 Do. Another without the name of Evenetus, varied.

These very much admired coins have not quite escaped criticism; the treatment of the hair is a little mannered, and Mr Poole notes other imperfections.

Probably struck during the tyranny of the elder Dionysius 405—367 B. C.

131, 132 Do. Others, with the name of the artist Cimon (ΚΙΜΩΝ) inscribed on the lowest dolphin.

The hair of Proserpine is now confined in a net behind. Nothing can surpass the technical skill of all the details of these magnificent pieces. They may be referred to the age of the younger Dionysius (367—343 B. C.).

K. O. Müller calls the Syracusan medallions "the costly master-pieces of Sicilian engravers." (*Ancient art and its remains.*)

133 Do. Copper coin. *Obv.* ΣΤΡΑ-ΚΟΣΙΩΝ. Head of Proserpine. *Rev.* Biga, above it a star. In the exergue uncertain traces of letters (probably ΠΟ. Χ., as in a similar coin described by Mionnet).

134 Do. Copper Uncia or Ounce. *Obv.* ΣΤΡΑ. Head of Pallas to left, in Corinthian helmet, around it an olive-wreath. *Rev.* Star between opposite dolphins.

The full weight of these Sicilian ounces is thought by Leake to have been about 500 Troy grains; and their age to be about that of Dionysius I. They are heavier than the ancient Roman ounces in the proportion of 25 to 21.

135 Do. Copper coin, on the reverse of which is an hippocamp or sea-horse, with a cord hanging from its mouth.

136 Do. Copper coin. *Obv.* ΣΤΡΑ-ΚΟΣΙΩΝ. Head of Hercules in lion's scalp to left. *Rev.* Pallas in forked drapery, in field owl.

This is interesting as being a re-struck coin (nummus recusus); the new types were impressed on a common coin of Agathocles (n. 139), and the types and legends of his coin are still in part visible. Hence we infer that the present coin is at least as late as Agathocles; probably it is later.

Tyrants of Syracuse.

No genuine coins of any tyrants of Syracuse before Agathocles, which bear their name, are in existence; even under the Dionysii the republican forms were observed, and the coins read ΣΤΡΑΚΟΣΙΩΝ; and it is probable that a great part of the copper money which has the same legend is later than Agathocles; in some instances we know for certain that it cannot be earlier; see n. 136.

137 Agathocles (317—289 B.C.). Gold coin, apparently of six litræ.

This would seem by the weight to be a piece of six litræ.

138 Do. Silver tetradrachm.

The obverse (inscribed ΚΟΡΑΣ) is the head of Proserpine as usual. The trophy of the reverse consists of an upright stake against which are nailed a breast-plate and various pieces of armour.

139 Do. Copper coin.

The Doric form of the genitive in 137, 139 may be noted; ΑΓΑΘΟΚΛΕΙΟΣ in 138 agrees with νεώμμος or some such word; cf. n. 124.

140 Hicetas (289—279 B.C.). Gold drachma.

141 Hiero II. (270—216 B.C.). Gold drachma.

142 Do. Silver piece of 88 litræ, = 6½ Attic drachms (Lagid octo-drachm, according to Queipo).

The portrait on this and the two following coins is probably that of Hiero II. himself.

143 Do. Copper coin.

144 Do. Copper ounce. See n. 134.

145 Gelo II., son of the preceding, and associated with him in the government. Died before his father. Silver piece of eight litræ (or, in Queipo's view, a Lagid drachma).

Obs. Portrait of Gelon II. to left. *Rev.* ΣΤΡΑΚΟΣΙΟΙ ΓΕΛΩΝΟΣ. Victory in a biga to right.

The construction is difficult. Probably ΓΕΛΩΝΟΣ is merely the ordinary regal genitive, not depending on ΣΤΡΑΚΟΣΙΟΙ; these (the citizens) seem to be symbolized by the victorious type of the reverse.

146, 147 Philistis, supposed to be queen of Hiero II. Seems from the weight to be a piece of 15 litræ (Tetradrachm of the Lagid scale, according to Queipo).

Except on her coins, her name only occurs in an inscription on the great theatre of Syracuse, where it is associated with Nereis, queen of Gelon II.

148 Hieronymus (216—215 B.C.). Silver didrachm, or decalitron.

The portrait is probably Hieronymus himself. Leake prefers to regard the portraits on coins of Hiero II., Gelon II., and Hieronymus as meant for Gelon I. It is more likely that they were a great family likeness between Hiero II. and his two sons Gelon II. and Hieronymus; similarly the portraits of Vespasian, Titus, and Domitian are very similar.

149 Tauromenium (Taormina). Gold litra, apparently: but heavy.

150 Do. Silver-piece of four litræ.

151 Do. Copper coin, on which Apollo bears the title ΑΡΧΑΓΕΤΑΣ.

Tauromenium in 358 B.C. received the remaining inhabitants of Naxos (in Sicily); and the Naxians, on the foundation of their city from Chalcis in Eubœa, brought with them a statue of Apollo Archegetes, as the founder of the colony.

DIVISION V.

ISLANDS OF THE EGEAN, &c.   AFRICAN GREECE.

§ 1. *Islands of the Egean sea with Cyprus.*

1—9 Ægina.

At this place, according to Ephorus and most Greek authorities, silver money was first coined by Pheidon, king of Argos, about 740 B.C. Hence emanated the Eginetan scale, which to judge by the coins, had for its principal division a drachma weighing about 93 grains Troy, which was subdivided into 6 obols. Nos. 1 and 2 are probably among the earliest coins in existence, and scarcely differ from ingots; they may be referred to the 7th or perhaps even 8th century B.C. A rude sea-tortoise is the type of one side; and a rude punch mark disfigures the other side. These coins are didrachms, as is also n. 3, which has the same types, but is of a later though very early date, being probably of the 6th century B.C. The workmanship of both sides is much less rude. No. 4 is an hemidrachm. Nos. 5 and 6 are respectively a didrachm and obol of the later type, a land-tortoise; nos. 7 and 8 are an obol and half-obol of the older form. The Eginetan drachma soon declined to about 88 grains.

9　Carthæa of Ceos. Silver didrachm of the later debased Attic standard (of about 60 grains to the drachma).

Aristæus (who long dwelt in Ceos) implored Jupiter and Sirius (the dog-star) to cause a plague in Greece to cease; hence probably the type of the dog-star. Leake considers this coin to be of about the first century B.C.

10　Chalcis of Eubœa. Drachma of Queipo's Bosporic scale, which appears to be the Euboic scale of antiquity. See note at the end.

The Euboic scale is still uncertain, and Mr Poole thinks that the coins of Eubœa have been the main hindrance to its discovery. See Smith's *Dict. of the Bible*, vol. 3, under *Weights*.

11　Chios. Very early drachma. Bosporic scale.

The pointed form of the amphora may be noted, which came down even to Roman times.

12　Do. Tetradrachm, same scale.

13　Do. A copper coin declaring itself to be a three-as piece!

These pieces are probably of the third century after Christ, and have been referred to the reign of Gallienus. The Roman as originally weighed a pound, which seems not to have differed very much from the pound Troy (the former is variously estimated, by Böckh at 5053 grains; the latter weighs 5760 grains;) now however three asses weigh about as much as a heavy English penny.

14　Crete in genere, of Caligula. Silver didrachm, of debased Attic scale, apparently.

15　Cnossus in Crete, with a square labyrinth. Drachma of the Eginetan scale, which prevailed in Crete generally, for the earlier coins.

16　Do. with circular labyrinth. Tetradrachm of Bosporic scale.

The different modes of representing the same labyrinth, shews that a certain conventionality must be looked for in architectural and other representations on coins. A cavern, partly natural, partly artificial, still exists near Gortyna; the reputed work of Dædalus. This is probably the labyrinth of the present coin.

17　Corcyra (Corfu). Probably a light Eginetan didrachm. *Obv.* Cow to left and calf to right, sucking her. *Rev.* A type which has been commonly supposed to represent the gardens of Alcinous, on one side K.

Similar types occur on coins of Dyrrhachium and Apollonia, colonies of Corinth. See Div. III. nos 13 and 59.

18　Do. Reduced Attic hemidrachm, apparently.

The Pegasus is a reminiscence of Corinth, the mother city of Corcyra.

19　Do. having a crater on the obverse. Probably a tetrobol of reduced Attic scale.

20　Cos. Tetradrachm (Attic) of fine old work.

The dancing figure is probably Apollo.

21　Corœsia in Ceos. Eginetan didrachm of very early work.

6

For the form of the incuse, compare the coins of Ægina, nos. 2 and 8.

22 Cydonia in Crete. Eginetan didrachm, fine work.

The Cydonians were renowned for the use of the bow.

Tela Cydonio direxit arcu. Hor. *Od.* IV. 9.

23 Commune Cypri, under Caracalla. Copper coin.

For an account of the temple of Venus at Paphos, whose image is a conical stone, seen in the centre of the reverse, see Donaldson's *Architectura Numismatica,* n. 31.

24 Cyprus of Claudius. Copper coin, struck "under Cominius Proclus, proconsul."

This is the most important of all coins for establishing the accuracy of the New Testament, where there seemed grave reason to suspect an error. St Luke had termed Sergius Paulus, the ἀνθύπατος or proconsul of Cyprus; and it was thought by Grotius and others that he ought to have called him ἀντιστράτηγος or propraetor. The present coin shews that, in the time of Claudius, Cyprus was governed by a proconsul (ἀνθύπατος), whose name was Cominius Proclus, and therefore that the term used by the Evangelist is correct. It had previously been governed by a propraetor, but in the time of Augustus an exchange of provinces took place between the emperor and the Senate, and consequently the title of the presiding governor was then changed; the ἀνθύπατος, being the title of the governor of the Senatorial provinces, as δευτεραγωγός was of that of the Imperial. See Akerman's *Numismatic Illustrations of the New Testament;* Paley's *Evidences,* part II. c. VI. § 6.

25 Gortyna in Crete. Eginetan didrachm, of very early work.

The very archaic characters stand for ΓΟΡΤΥΝΟΣ ΤΟ ΣΑΙΜΑ (ΣΗΜΑ). The lion's scalp was the παράσημον, coat of arms, so to say, of Gortyna; and it is here termed σῆμα. "The style and letters indicate a production of the sixth century B.C." (Leake.)

26 Do. Tetradrachm of (somewhat reduced) Attic scale with Athenian types. See Div. III. nos. 25—27.

This rather late coin certainly indicates an alliance with Athens, when it was struck. Previously in the Peloponnesian war the cities had been allied; but the age of the present coin is probably that of Philip V. See *Num. Chron.* for 1861, p. 174.

27 Do. Eginetan didrachm.

Pliny's observation explains the type (xii. § 5): "Est Gortyna platanus ... statimque ei Graeciae fabulositas imperfuit, Jovem sub ea cum Europa concubuisse." The bull of the reverse is of course the bull of Europa.

28 Histiaea in Euboea. Probably a tetrobol of the Euboic scale. See Leake's *Notes on the weights of Greek coins* in the *Numismata Hellenica.*

The head of the obverse rather seems to be a Bacchante, than "Bacchi faemineum caput" (Eckhel); the female on the reverse is probably Histiaea, the foundress of the city.

29 Referred by Leake to Ialysus in Rhodes, but doubtless belonging to the Cyrenaica, probably to Cyrene itself. Attic tetradrachm.

This is n. 22 of Müller's *Cyrenaïque* (monnaies sans nom de ville), and it has given rise to some discussion. The eagle devouring a serpent is regarded as symbolical of victory, sent by Jove; and the lion's head has been conjectured to be a Samian type, placed on the coin by Arcesilas III. (B.C. 530—514), who recovered his kingdom by aid of the Samians. L. Müller considers that the style of the coin points to this date. *Numism. de l'anc. Afrique,* vol. I. p. 18. Compare Div. IV. n. 92, which probably suggested this view.

30 Itanus in Crete. Eginetan (reduced) drachma of fine work.

31 Ios. Copper coin, bearing the head of Homer (inscribed).

Other places, as Chios, Smyrna, and Amastris have placed Homer on their coins. Homer was reputed to be buried in Ios, one of the Cyclades.

32 Copper coin of Ithaca, bearing the head, as is thought, of Ulysses.

33 Lesbos. Small early coin of base silver or potin. Apparently half-hecta of the Cyzicene or Phocaean stater.

34 Lyttus in Crete. Early drachma of the Eginetan scale, reduced.

The forms of the letters T and O are remarkable. This is but little heavier than a drachma of the so-called Olympic scale; which seems to be the Eginetan scale reduced.

35 Do. Eginetan didrachm; later, but early (probably of the fifth century B.C.).

36 Mytilene. Hecta of Cyzicene or Phocaean stater. The M of the reverse above the calf's head, the type of Mytilene, leaves little doubt of the attribution. Leake thinks the female head is Diana.

37 Do. Coin of potin, with remarkable quadrate incuse.

38 Do. Do., but lighter.

Leake thinks that the exact resemblance in form, style, and material, and in the size and form of their reverse leaves little doubt that they were struck in the same city. The weights however are different, and it is hazardous to pronounce on their denominations: no. 36 may perhaps be a light Eginetan drachm, while no. 37 appears to be a Rhosperic or Lagid tetradrachm.

39 Naxus (in the Egean Sea). Heavy Eginetan didrachm of very early work, of the age of Darius Hystaspes, as Leake thinks.

A very ancient representation of the cantharus, which retains the present form (or nearly so) in the Greek-Italian vases of the Decadence.

40 Olus in Crete. Eginetan didrachm.

The head is probably from the statue of Diana Britomartis at Olus, mentioned by Pausanias. The more coins are studied, the more it appears that they preserve many copies from ancient statues. The wreath of ivy on Diana's head is unusual.

41 Phaestus in Crete. Eginetan didrachm.

42 Do. Do.

The fine vase in the field is the *enidor* or peculiar cup of Hercules. Cf. Div. IV. n. 22.

43 Do. Do.

These coins exhibiting Hercules as the slayer of the serpent of the Hesperides, as the assailant of the Hydra, and as reposing after his labours, well illustrate Mr Poole's remark that the Cretan artists make their coins more pictorial and more full in details than we find elsewhere.

44 Polyrhenium in Crete. Eginetan didrachm (rather light).

This is an early coin to bear a magistrate's name in full. The O (not Ω) in the legend shows that it is not much later than B.C. 400, while the occurrence of H equally shows that it is not much earlier.

45 Priansus in Crete. Eginetan didrachm.

46 Rhodes. Tetradrachm of Bosporic (or Euboic) scale; see below, no. 69.

The flower on the reverse is certainly the rose (not the pomegranate, as Leake and many others); this is put out of all doubt by the divided sepals. For the various scales of the money of Rhodes see Queipo, tab. XXXII.

47 Do. Didrachm of the same scale.

48 Do. Do.

49 Do. Tetrobol, apparently.

50 Do. Copper medallion.

The fine execution of the head of Bacchus, as well as of his ivy crown, deserves attention, in a copper coin more especially.

51 Nicocles, king of Salamis in Cyprus. Succeeded his father Evagoras I. B.C. 374; time of his death unknown. Eginetan drachma.

The BA of the obverse and the NIK of the reverse (in monogram) are an abbreviation for ΒΑΣΙΛΕΩΣ ΝΙΚΟΚΛΕΟΣ, or (as Leake prefers) ΒΑΣΙΛΕΩΣ ΝΙΚΟΚΛΕΟΤΣ.

6—2

This coin might better have been placed under Div. I., and the same remark may be made of nos. 137—148 in the Div. IV., and of some others; but it has been thought advisable to follow the order of the *Numismata Hellenica* for the convenience of reference in all cases.

52 Samos, island of Ionia. Attic te-tradrachm.

These ordinary Samian types (lion's scalp and fore-part of bull) occur also upon coins of Rhegium and Messana, Div. IV. n. 92, q. v.

53 Do. Apparently a light tetra-drachm of the Greco-Asiatic (or Rhodian) scale.

Similar types occur on coins of Rhodes and Ephesus, and indicate an alliance between the three cities.

54 Do. of Domitian. Small copper coin.

55 Do. of Philip, junior. Large do.

The Samian Juno, which appears on these coins, may be compared with the Ephesian Diana. Div. II. no. 32, &c.

A bronze statuette of the Samian Juno, found near her temple, agrees (substantially) with the representations on the coins; a plaster cast may be seen in the Leake collection in the sculpture room.

56 Soli, on the coast of Cilicia. Double siclos of the Persian scale, but light.

In Div. II. no. 81 we have an example of the Siclos (σίκλος), the unit of this scale, in a coin of Sardes in Lydia: it weighs about 85 grains.

N.B. This coin has by inadvertence been placed here, and not under Division II., Soli not being on an island.

57 Tenedos, island of the Egean. Tetradrachm of the Attic scale.

58 Thasos, island of the Egean, near Thrace. Eginetan didrachm.

The attribution of this coin is uncertain. Sestini (*Descriz. degli stateri antichi*, p. 20, Fir. 1817), assigns it to Phocæa; Mionnet leaves

it uncertain. Copper coins of Ægina bear a dolphin, and the reverse of this coin resembles those of Ægina; nevertheless Leake's attribution is as plausible as any other.

59 Ditto. Tetradrachm, apparently of the Bosporic (or Euboic) scale, but heavy. See Div. I. no. 1.

The ivy wreath on the head of Bacchus, on this and the following coin, is remarkably graceful; and Mr Ruskin observes that it rather resembles a growth than a composition.

60 Do. Drachma of the same scale, also heavy.

Queipo would probably regard this and the preceding as belonging to "le système attique, affaibli de poids," tab. xxxiii. The great antiquity however of the coins makes this view less probable.

61 Do. Later tetradrachm, Attic scale.

62 Do. Barbarous imitation of the above.

63 Do. Apparently an obolus of the Eginetan scale.

As Thasos was not always under the same masters, it is not wonderful that its coins are not all of one scale.

§ 2. African Greece.

64 Barca in the Cyrenaica. Tetra-drachm of the Greco-Asiatic (or Rhodian) scale.

Botanists are not all agreed about the Silphium plant, so generally represented on the money of the Cyrenaica. That it is an umbelliferous plant seems certain, but whether a Thapsia, a Laserpitium, or a Ferula is doubtful. L. Müller concludes thus: "Il est probable que le silphium appartenu au genre *Ferula;* c'est ce qu'on peut conclure du fruit figuré sur les monnaies." *Num. d'anc Afrique*, vol. I. p. 108.

With regard to the monetary scale, he writes: "Le système monétaire est le même qui était adopté à Cyrène à cette époque (B. C. 450 —86). La presque totalité des monnaies de Barca appartient au système que nous avons appelé Asiatique." p. 87. For the various opinions about this scale, see p. 119.

65 Do. Do., with the head of Jupiter Ammon seen full face.

The Jupiter Ammon is probably an Egyptian deity the Lord of Heaven (Amun-Ra); one of whose forms is Amun-nef or Amun-Chnufis. His image at Thebes and elsewhere is represented with ram's horns, as the protector of flocks. His temple and oracle (Ammonium) in the Oasis was equally resorted to by Egyptians, Ethiopians, and Greeks; and was visited by Alexander, who figures on various coins as the young Ammon. See Div. t. nos. 20, 33, &c. See Müller as above, pp. 94—104.

66 Cyrene. Gold stater of the Attic scale (Müller); this specimen weighs above 132 grains.

Leake takes Polianthus on the reverse of this coin to be an epithet of the Jove who holds a phiale over a candelabrum; L. Müller considers it to be the name of a magistrate (p. 71). These coins he considers to be of the fourth century B.C.

67 Do. Probably half-quarter of the Attic gold stater, but possibly a hecta of a different scale (see L. Müller, p. 71).

By JOHN'S COLLEGE, CAMBRIDGE,
July 8, 1867.

The female head (not "young male head") of the reverse is probably the nymph Cyrene. See Müller, p. 52.

68 Do. Tetradrachm of the Greco-Asiatic (Rhodian Scale.)

69 Do. Didrachm of Bosporic (or Eubolc) scale, termed by L. Müller Phenician (p. 119).

For the different views about the scale, see Müller as above. It is heavier than the Greco-Asiatic, lighter than the Attic; Müller includes therein the two scales termed by Queipo Bosporic and Lagid; it has been already suggested Div. t. no. 1 and no. 97, and Div. v. no. 10 and no. 28, that these may be Euboic.

With regard to the young horned head (or young Ammon), Müller writes, p. 101: "Cette tête représente sans doute un dieu libyco-grec, le fils d'Ammon assimilé au fils de Jupiter, auquel on peut, avec le plus de raison, donner le nom de Bacchus libyen."

70 Silver denarius of Trajan, presumed to belong to the Cyrenaica.

The coin was struck A.D. 100. L. Müller does not consider the attribution of this and similar coins certain (p. 173).

CHURCHILL BABINGTON.

Note on the Weights of Greek Coins.

Queipo's system of monetary weights is divided into seven scales; assuming the French gramme = 15,434 grains Troy, the unit or drachma of each scale in Troy grains is, in his view, as follows, beginning with the lightest, and ascending up to the heaviest:

Greco-Asiatic	30.14
Lagid	54.02
Bosporic	57.24
Attic	83.07
Olympic	73.29
Persian	83.93
Commercial Attic	90.49

Besides these he counts the Rhodian scale, which he considers to be the double of the Greco-Asiatic; and the Septuagintal scale, which is the double of the Lagid. Notwithstanding all that has been done for Greek metrology before and since the appearance of his Essai in 1859, little is finally and satisfactorily made out, beyond the determination of the Attic scale of Solon, and its subsequent degradation. Col. Leake makes the normal Attic drachma a little heavier (67.5 Troy grains); but observes that in the 1st century B.C. it had fallen down to about 60 grains. This declension explains the remark of the later Latin writers (Pliny, &c.), who make the Attic drachma equivalent to the Roman denarius of their own time. In the same way there seems to be a tendency in all the other scales to decline; just as in the English scale the pennyweight of the tables is 24 grains Troy—and there are pennies of Alfred of this weight—whereas the shilling of Victoria (excluding the alloy of 18 pennyweights per lb,) weighs 80,7$\frac{2}{7}$ grains, thus giving something less than 7 grains to the pennyweight. This circumstance, added to the carelessness or fraud of those who were employed to strike coins in ancient times, makes a subject, which in itself is far from simple, in a much higher degree complicated. It may be sufficient to mention here that the tetradrachms of Alexander the Great, all of which were struck according to the Attic scale of Solon, and therefore normally weighing 270 grains, do in fact vary between 274 and 254 grains, or less, in well-preserved specimens (*Num. Chron.* for 1864, pp. 2, 3). The loss of weight by friction and chemical action is an additional element of difficulty in determining the scales of ancient coins. Consequently the scale of the smaller coins is usually more doubtful than that of the larger. It must be borne in mind that all the coins of the same king or of the same city are not necessarily adjusted to the same scale, even when the metal is the same. The gold and the silver money of the same king or city frequently belong to different scales. A few remarks are subjoined, not without great hesitation, on the above scales of Queipo.

1. Greco-Asiatic scale, widely prevalent in Asia. (See Brandis' recent work mentioned below.) Certain Rhodian coins also are adjusted to this scale, but the Rhodian denominations are considered by Queipo to be double the value of the Greco-Asiatic, so that a Greco-Asiatic drachma of about 50 grains would be a Rhodian hemidrachm. This opinion, however, seems doubtful. Pinder with greater reason considers the Rhodian scale synonymous with that of the *Cistophori,* i.e. with the Greco-Asiatic (*Ueber die Cistophoren,* p. 531). Brandis in fine estimates the Rhodian didrachm at 15.60 grammes, which gives 120.39 grains for the Rhodian drachm, instead of Queipo's 100,25. This system obtains not only in many of the Greco-Asiatic towns, but also in Northern Europe and Africa. See Div. i. no. 34, and Div. v. no. 64.

2 and 3. Legid (which might better be termed Ptolemaic) and Bosporic scales. These are so nearly the same, that they had better be regarded as variations of one scale, lying between 55 and 58 grains for the drachma. This is by some, as by L. Müller, termed Phœnician. Col. Leake is inclined to think that it is the scale known to antiquity as the Euboic, as the coins of Chalcis in Eubœa give a drachma of about 56 grains. It obtains in Macedonia and elsewhere, and was thence derived to the Ptolemies, under whom it was slightly reduced (55 grains). See Div. i. no. 1, and Div. v. no. 69.

4. Attic, as settled at the reform of Solon; the principal Attic coins, and their weights in Troy grains (taken from Leake's estimate), are subjoined.

Drachm, 67,5.

Of this the principal multiples are:

Didrachm, 135.

Tetradrachm, 270.

The obol is one-sixth of the drachma, and weighs 11,25 grains. The double, triple, quadruple, of this are called the diobol (22,5), triobol (33,75), and tetrobol (45). The half-obol is the principal fraction of the obol, and weighs 5,62 grains. The Attic scale, in a more or less reduced form, became at length almost universal.

At Corinth the standard coin or stater was equal to the Attic didrachm; and it was divided into 10 litræ, each weighing 13,5 grains. This variety of the Attic scale may be well studied in the coins of Syracuse.

The larger gold coins of Sardis, the gold Darics, the Attic gold and silver didrachms, and the Corinthian silver staters are all of about the same weight (135—132 grains Troy); the Egyptian monad or unit of weight being also said by Horapollo to be equivalent to the Attic didrachm; a unit which may be derived from Babylon, the mother-country, according to some, of weights and measures.

The double of this Egyptian or Babylonian unit occurs in the double Daric; also in the gold and electrum staters of Cyzicus and Phocæa, which were commonly divided into sixths or hectæ. Some, as Brandis, make these a distinct scale (*Phokaischer Fuss*).

5. Olympic scale. This scale of 75 grains to the drachma is by some writers, as by L. Müller and Poole, considered as the Æginetan scale of antiquity; and it may not without reason be looked upon as a reduced though very

ancient form of that scale, connected by various links with the Commercial Attic of authors, which is for Col. Leake and for the writer of this note the true Eginetan scale; giving about 93 grains to the drachma. It obtains in various parts of northern Greece, Crete, Asia Minor, &c. Queipo regards it as derived from the Bosporic scale.

6. Persian. The unit, or siclos, of about 84 grains, as well as the double of the same weight, is seen in the Persian Aryandica, and in many coins of Cilicia, Pamphylia and Pisidia (Div. II. no. 9, and Div. v. no. 50); likewise in the coins of Sardis in Lydia, so far as the silver coinage is concerned.

7. Commercial Attic. The drachma of this scale (which in the earliest coins of Ægina weighs about 95 grains, but in the later coins of the same island diverends to about 80 grains), is estimated by Queipo at 90 grains. Leake and Brandis seem to be right in regarding this scale as Eginetan; which prevails both in Ægina and the Peloponnese, and also in Crete and parts of Asia, as Teos. This likewise seems to have been the original scale at Athens before Solon's reform (though no ancient Athenian coins, it is believed, of this standard are known, having been probably all or nearly all melted), and his establishment of the Attic didrachm at 135 grains was with the view of assimilating the Attic weights of coins to those of other countries.

This scale continued in use at Athens, after the Solonian reformation, for commercial though not for monetary use; much as among ourselves Troy weight is in use for the precious metals, but avoirdupois weight for most other commodities.

The preceding remarks apply to coins of gold (or electrum) and silver exclusively; the copper coins of Greece do not seem to have been struck according to any fixed scales, but rather to have been tokens, so to say, issued by the state. In Italy the case was different, where the heavy as, of one pound weight, was the unit; in Sicily also we have the ounces (see Div. IV. n. 134), which must have been a coin of sterling value. In Egypt, likewise, are some very heavy copper coins issued by the Ptolemies, as well as by Antiochus IV. (see Div. I. n. 32), to which we must assign a real value. Many of the coins of Magna Græcia and Sicily bear globules indicating the number of unciæ or twelfths of the Roman as, for which they were current, but the as was then very much reduced from its original weight, and in process of time a three-as piece became no heavier than an English penny of George III. Coins of the Roman empire are usually divided into First or Large brass, Second or Middle brass, Third or Small brass; the First brass being regarded as a sestertce (or two asses and a half), the Second brass as a Dupondius, the Third brass as an as. Those which are larger than the average of the First brass are vaguely termed Medallions. The same expression is also applied to silver coins of the empire, which exceed the usual imperial size (i.e. that of the denarius, which weighed about 60 grains, for the early emperors, but fell at length to about 50 grains), of which there are examples in Div. II. nos. 30, 55, 98; and it is similarly applied to Greek silver coins which exceed in weight the ordinary large size or tetradrachm. Thus the decadrachm of Syracuse are often called Syracusan medallions; see Div. IV. nos. 128—132. The word *medal* is now employed by English numismatic writers at least to denote a commemorative piece in whatever metal, which was never destined to circulate as money; of which there are abundance from the fifteenth century to our own time, but in ancient times such pieces scarcely existed at all. (Some, however, have regarded the Syracusan medallions as prize-medals.) The only piece exhibited in this selection which can be regarded as a medal is a gold piece of Macedonia, Div. III. n. 80, the genuineness of which is doubtful.

In addition to the works on Greek metrology mentioned by Mr Poole, in his valuable article on *Weights and Measures*, in Smith's *Dict. of the Bible*, vol. III. pp. 1727–1731, it may be worth while to add, *Notes on the Weights of Greek coins* in an appendix to Col. Leake's *Numismata Hellenica*, and the same writer's paper on Syracuse in the *Transactions of the Royal Society of Literature* for 1830; also L. Müller's *Numism. de l'anc. Afrique*, vol. I. pp. 114–125. Copenhagen, 1860; and a book which has just appeared at Berlin (1866) by J. Brandis, entitled *Das Mûns-Mass-und Gewichtswesen in vorderasien bis auf Alexander den Grosses*, of which less use has been made in compiling this catalogue than perhaps might have been, had it come to the knowledge of the compiler earlier.

* 9 7 8 3 7 4 2 8 2 5 3 6 0 *